Betty

The Autobiography

Betty
The Autobiography

Betty Driver

WITH

Daran Little

GRANADA
MEDIA

First published in 2000 by Granada Media
an imprint of André Deutsch Ltd
in association with
Granada Media Group
76 Dean Street
London W1V 5HA
www.vci.co.uk

A catalogue record for this book is available from
the British Library

ISBN 0 233 99780 6

Typeset by Derek Doyle & Associates, Liverpool
Printed and bound in the UK by
Mackays of Chatham

1 3 5 7 9 10 8 6 4 2

Plate section design by Design 23

This book is dedicated to my sister, Freda, to whom
I owe everything

Contents

Prologue

There have been plenty of things in my life that I wish had never happened but out of them all I have only one real regret. I never wanted to work in variety, that old-fashioned art form that found singers, comics, acrobats and dancers trying desperately to please theatres full of the public who had paid good money to be entertained: twice nightly, six days a week, travelling to the next venue on Sunday, then another opening, another show. I did it for over twenty years, until the lights were dimmed in the theatres and television enticed the audiences to stay at home. Over twenty years, and I hated every day of it.

When I was still young enough to question what I was doing I tried to convince my mother I would much prefer to work in a florist's or train to be a hairdresser. We were standing at the side of a stage and the compère had just announced, 'Betty Driver, the Dynamic Singing Star!' The orchestra had started up with my intro. The conversation went something like this:

Me: 'Mam, do I have to go on?'

Mam: 'Give over Betty!'

Me: 'Mam, I mean it. I'm so nervous . . .'

SLAP

Mam: 'Get on that stage! And don't forget to smile!'

And I went on, a great red five-fingered hand-mark across my cheek, and started to sing my first number with tears rolling down my face. I glanced to the side and my mother was there in the wings, where she always stood, watching me, her mouth moving as she sang along quietly with me, her hands mirroring my gestures, her legs moving to my steps. Oh, Mam, why couldn't you have gone on in my place?

CHAPTER ONE

A Little Family Background

As I've started with Mother I ought to introduce her properly. Her name was Nellie Driver, and she was a small woman with a strident voice. She was born in 1899 in Leicester to parents who were chalk and cheese. Her father, a professional sportsman called William Bridgeford, was a lovely man, from a good family. He was slim, had fair hair and blue eyes, very handsome. He used to enter competitions with his garden produce and always won at flower shows. He was athletic too and at one time played football for Leicester City. His marriage to Grandmother was unhappy. She dominated him, and I suppose my mother followed her lead.

Grandmother's name was Louisa. She was tall and striking, with jet-black hair and bright blue eyes. Grandfather loved her, but she couldn't have cared less about him. She always wore black, from head to foot, and once my sister Freda asked her why. She said, 'I'm mourning for my lost love.'

She was from good stock: her family name was Cox and her mother was a titled lady from the south who married a lawyer and lived in Chelsea. When he left her and their two daughters, of whom my grandmother was the youngest, to emigrate to Sydney, Australia, with his brother, it was arranged that she and the girls would live in a cottage in south Leicestershire with a maid. Off he went, but when he came back she was pregnant, by another man. He abandoned her and, from having been a cosseted girl, she was forced to take in laundry, and struggled to provide for her family.

After marrying Grandfather, Louisa moved to South Wigston, near Leicester, and brought up three daughters, Mabel, Nellie and Winifred.

Wigston Magna was a rural community neighbouring the larger town of South Wigston. It was three miles out of Leicester and was a gorgeous place. It boasted a tiny cinema and an old country church. For me it was the most beautiful place in the world and I loved to go there. The attraction was the neat house that was home to my other set of grandparents, George and Polly Driver. Their house had a long garden, which ran down to the church, and as children Freda and I would sit under the shade of fruit trees listening to the church bells ring. Grandfather George was an engine-driver and took the Royal Mail locomotive from London to Scotland, but his real passion in life was his garden. He grew enough fruit and vegetables to feed himself, his wife and ten children. If Freda and I weren't sitting under a tree we'd be in the tiny shed at the foot of the garden: it was here that he taught us, as he'd taught his children, how to clean shoes properly. He kept all the polish and brushes in the shed, along with all the bulbs and vegetables he was storing. We'd sit in there for hours, smelling the wonderful country smell, all mixed with boot polish.

George Driver was a well-built man of over six foot. He had steel-grey hair and a little pointed beard, which made him look like King George V. The thing I remember most about him was his hands – I was always asking him to show them to me. They were big and strong, very masculine with long fingers and beautifully shaped nails. When he was a young man, he had been a valet in a stately home in Leicestershire and Grandma was a maid in the same house. They got married and had a little cottage – a lodge house – in the grounds. King Edward VII used to come to see the master of the house and took a fancy to Grandma, so Grandfather decided he wasn't going to risk his wife's virtue: they left service and moved to Wigston.

As they had been in service, they were experts on household matters and taught us grandchildren everything they knew. They had beautiful table linen, and Grandfather liked to sit us at the table, get all the cutlery out and teach us how to set a table for dinner – seven or eight knives and forks, rows of glasses. We learned which glass was for which sort of wine, and about the different plates. Now I wouldn't be embarrassed to eat beside the Queen! They had beautiful cut glasses and old-fashioned cruet sets in solid silver, six bottles on a little turntable. These things had been gifts from the gentleman they'd worked for, but while some people might have locked them all away, my grandparents used them every day. The gentleman's wedding gift had been a whole dinner and tea service: fine china decorated with tiny violets, inside the cups and round the edges of the plates. When Grandma died not one piece had been broken – and she used it every day, with a stone sink to wash up.

If the garden was Grandfather's domain, the house was

Grandma's. She kept it spotless and tidy – I suppose with only three bedrooms and ten children growing up in it she had to! I remember it had glorious gas fittings with the most beautiful gas mantles, which cast warm shadows everywhere. On the dresser there'd be a jar full of boiled sweets and bottles of pop, and the whole house smelt of lavender. It was only a little stone terrace house: you went through the front door and there was a long passage, with a highly polished floor. Right at the end was the loo. It had a door with open-work on it in the shape of a heart. The toilet seat was pure white from scrubbing, and on one side Grandma hung little squares of paper she had cut up, while on the other was the family Bible. I'd sit there, looking out of a little window with the sun coming in. Outside the loo door there was a canary in a cage, singing its little heart out.

In the spring you'd look out of the sitting-room window on to a bed of lilies of the valley, three yards long and wide. On one side of the garden path there would be phlox, striped pink and white, and we'd sit by them, hypnotized by the scent. There were three or four rows of different currants and fruit bushes and Grandfather always managed to arrange for us to visit when the fruit was ripe. Before we'd got our coats off he'd take us down the garden and tell us from which bushes we could eat and which weren't yet ripe. I suppose it's from him that I've got my love of flowers. I adore them. I would rather buy flowers than have a meal. I spend whole days in garden centres.

Grandma was as short as Grandfather was tall. She was a little bird of a woman who got up at five o'clock each morning and by seven all her washing would be done. She was a character, the mainstay of the family. Her mother lived in a village nearby and she lived to be ninety-nine. On the eve of her hundredth birthday the vicar went to see her and said, 'Mrs Truman, the church bells will ring in the morning for your birthday,' and she said 'Why? They've never rung before. Why in the morning?' and he said, 'Because you're a hundred.' She couldn't believe it and the shock killed her: she died that night. My grandfather's mother lived to be 103. My grandfather lived to be eighty-seven. He died because the authorities felt he was too old for my grandma to look after him and took him into hospital, where he died. Shortly afterwards Grandma fell down the stairs and died too. She was eighty-eight.

My father, Frederick Andrew Driver, was six foot tall. When he was young, he was very slim and good-looking, with thick black hair and very dark eyes. He was a quiet soul, who wasn't at all demonstrative and never showed his feelings. He liked gardening and was interested in nature. He was a countryman and never really happy in the city. Just before the outbreak of war in 1914 he met my mother, then a beautiful girl of five foot four, slender, with natural ash-blonde hair. They fell in love and it was her letters that saved his life in the trenches when he was serving as a sergeant in the Leicestershire Division. He carried them in his breast pocket with a prayer book. He would have been killed when a bullet hit his chest but the letters diverted it into his arm. He came back to England, and when he had recovered he was sent to train other men. He was something of a crack shot, and they wanted him to stay in the Army after the war, but he'd already decided to marry Mother.

It seems funny to me to think of my parents as having been in love. I remember them bickering and fighting like cat and dog. Mother was outgoing and gregarious and quickly overshadowed my father. The thing was, he was content for her to take control: he was a man who liked discipline and related well to authority. I think Mother replaced his sergeant major! Left to himself he was lazy and had no ambition, unlike Mother who was constantly chasing dreams.

During the 1914–18 war Mother worked in a hosiery factory, but after becoming Mrs Frederick Driver on 26 July 1919, she gave up work and looked to my father to be the breadwinner. As well as working in the factory, she had also spent part of the war entertaining wounded soldiers on hospital pianos. She was a marvellous pianist and was self-taught – at the age of five she had played the church organ. I never saw her need music: she always played by ear. While she thumped out familiar tunes for the troops, something sparked in her: she discovered she enjoyed being centre-stage.

My father was also musical and played the violin. He had wanted to be a cellist but his father for some reason made him learn the violin. Unlike my mother he could read music, which led to rows whenever she played wrong notes.

There was a great deal of animosity between my parents' families. My father's parents refused to attend the wedding, saying my mother was too flighty to make a good wife. Father was saddened by this but wasn't deterred. Mother's parents were supportive and it was into their house in Leicester city centre that my father moved as a newly-wed. It was a terrible way to start a marriage as Grandmother Louisa started to boss him around in the same way as she bossed her own husband. Father was docile enough not to mind but Mother resented the interference: if anyone was going to tell her husband what to do it would be her.

CHAPTER TWO

Childhood

I made my first public appearance on 20 May 1920. When I was born after a sixteen-hour labour, my mother lay back in bed and vowed, 'Never again. I don't want another one like her,' as she lay under the crisp white sheet on a hard bed at the Prebend Nursing Home in Leicester. During the pregnancy she hadn't stopped eating oranges, which Father fetched from the market. She ate and ate, and ate, and I entered the world weighing twelve pounds – a great big lump of a screaming baby, who was named Betty Mary Driver, Mary after my father's beloved mother, which was odd because everyone called her Polly. The inclusion of his mother's name was my father's only involvement with me as a baby. As soon as Mother came home with her new-born bundle, Father was shoved into the background by my doting Grandmother Louisa. I didn't stand a chance, and within hours I was spoilt rotten.

As Grandmother Louisa clucked around me, indulging my every coo and gurgle, Father started to sneak off to public houses in search of masculine company. However, under Grandmother Louisa's care, I continued to demand and scream, so sometimes she would hand me over reluctantly to my father, who took me for walks in my pram, under the trees, and talked to me in a way that calmed me.

I wish he'd stood up to Mother. If he had, I'm certain she would not have been as domineering as she became, but he never did. From the moment I was born, until nineteen years later, when my sister Freda dared to stand against her, my mother was the driving force in my life. She was a shrewd, ambitious woman, and soon after my birth realized that her marriage would only survive if she removed us all from the clutches of her overbearing mother.

Father had been working as a trainee manager in a family-run hosiery factory. He wasn't suited to this, preferring to accept orders than give them. Eventually Mother took matters into her hands and suggested he joined the police force. Father liked the idea of wearing a uniform and working in an authoritarian environment – it sounded rather like the Army but without the enemy fire. He duly applied and was taken on as a constable in Manchester. That suited Mother: it was a fair distance from her parents and the thriving city would offer her as many distractions as she wanted.

After the First World War there was an aerodrome in leafy West Didsbury, a town to the south of Manchester surrounded by open fields and clusters of Victorian houses. The police force wanted to boost their presence in the area so this aerodrome was turned into a police community. There were some long wooden huts, like chalets, which had been workshops, and these were turned into makeshift homes for the new policemen and their families. We lived in hut number six and were an inharmonious family. Father worked the longest shifts he could, just to keep out of the hut.

Mother's plans for nights out at the cinema, the theatre and for fancy-dress parties were short-lived: she discovered she was pregnant again. She probably wouldn't have minded so much if I hadn't been such a swine as an infant, but robbed of the attention of Grandmother Louisa I had been unbearable, shouting and screaming all day and night. Mother said, 'If I have another like her I'll kill myself!' On five occasions she tried to bring on a miscarriage but the baby clung to life, determined to be born.

When that moment came, Manchester was living through one of the cruellest winters on record. Father had to run through the snow and sleet in the middle of the night to fetch the nurse and I had to be tied up and shoved into a cupboard because I was getting under everyone's feet, bawling and demanding attention. This was the family that Freda was born into on 12 January 1923. When I was freed from my prison and brought into the bedroom to see the horrid pink monkey, I looked down on her and hated her. Mother had no interest in her new daughter, and stunned the nurse by saying she wasn't bothered what she was called. The nurse suggested Freda, after my father Frederick, so Freda she became and has always hated her name.

I was terribly jealous of the new arrival: I was no longer the youngest and now someone else was making demands upon my parents' time. When I wasn't tormenting Freda – stealing her dummy, pinching her to make her cry – I'd be out playing around the aerodrome with our dog, a beautiful collie called Bess. I used to ride her like a pony and was madly in love with her. With Father at work and Mother stuck with the baby, I ran wild with the other police children, tearing around the open spaces. It was a stable period that lasted eighteen months, until the council completed building an estate off Platt Lane to house the police community. We were allocated a three-bedroomed semi-detached house, 18 Bucklow Avenue. It was my mother's first 'proper' home of her own, and before we moved in she decided to make one alteration to the family. The police warned her that a kennel wouldn't be allowed, and that Bess would have to live in the house. She wasn't having that and sold her. I was heartbroken as my dog was dragged away in front of me while Mother held me back to stop me running after her. Bess was my first pet, and since then I have always loved animals. All of them. Animals love you for yourself, not because of who you are. You don't have to be wealthy or famous, they just love you.

Our new home had big gardens to the front and rear. It was part of an estate of identical houses, all occupied by police families. Father indulged his passion for gardening and Mother left him to it. She enjoyed the bustle of living near main roads, with Manchester's busy social life just a tram-ride away. However, Freda and I followed Father into the garden. He taught us the names of the flowers and we each had our own little patch of earth to tend. Freda used to disappear into the back garden, sit in the middle of a big patch of mint and talk to fairies. Mother had no imagination and thought she was touched.

Generally Mother wasn't very domesticated but she was a fabulous cook and Freda spent happy hours helping her in the kitchen. However, her lessons in baking sent her back into the garden, where she made cakes out of mud and sold them to the local children in return for stones!

We'd always had a piano, an upright, which had been a wedding present to Mother from her parents. Sometimes, as a treat, she'd settle down and play while Father joined in with his violin. I loved those rare sessions of harmony – both musical and domestic. Mother encouraged me to sing along to her playing but ignored Freda's attempts. I was a confident child and loved singing, but was less happy when Mother decided to pay for me to have piano lessons. Freda, on the other hand, was a natural and longed for tuition: from an early age she had adored classical music and opera because it was played on the wireless at home. She'd sit entranced by it and mimic the singers. I was never interested in that sort of music and neither was Mother, who liked me to sing chirpy little numbers.

When I started my piano lessons, I was forced to learn scales and tunes, and loathed it but when Freda, who was only five, tickled the keys the piano-teacher recognized she had talent. She told Mother that Freda was a natural and offered to teach her for nothing, but Mother refused to let her and threw her out of the house. I can't explain why she was like that, why she concentrated on me and ignored Freda. Years later, when I was the family breadwinner, singing my heart out on stage, Freda and I would think it ironic that I'd never wanted to sing and she'd longed for nothing else. It was as if Freda had never been born. She was never nurtured.

Mother was stage-struck and the only way I can explain her behaviour is to say she wanted to live out her ambitions through me. She loved crude little variety numbers and I had a big voice so she pushed me. If she'd had a passion for classical music she would probably have pushed Freda instead.

School was at Wilbraham Road, round the corner from home. Again, it was filled with the children of policemen and we all knew each other. I loved school but can't remember much about it, except that I was a dreadful tomboy and used to fight the lads. After a while Freda joined me at the school and ended up in the same class as one Patricia Pilkington, who changed her name one day to Phoenix and drank the gins I served her over the bar at the Rovers Return.

My parents did not believe in celebrating birthdays or Christmas. I don't know why – it wasn't for any religious reason and it wasn't because they were mean or intended to be cruel, it was just something they didn't believe in. I'm ashamed to say that when I was growing up I could never work out how old I was as 20 May was just like any other day and had no special meaning for me. Freda was the same. She had no idea her twenty-first birthday had come and gone until months later! I only knew I was eighteen because I was working on a film at the time and the publicity department looked it up on my file.

When I was six, my father's parents bought Freda and me a pair of skates to share. Those skates were our only bought toys. We'd make dolls out of bits of old fabric and sneak across the street to Mrs Hodgkinson's house and be fed cake and read Tiger Tim in her children's comics.

Toys were like signs of affection: absent from our lives. We were never hugged or kissed, and while Dad never laid a finger on us Mother often lashed out with hard slaps. This affected Freda so much that she became very withdrawn and wouldn't speak to anybody; she was always being told, 'Shut your mouth and just sit there.'

Although Mother was quick to issue orders, my parents never laid down any rules so Freda and I were told off for doing something and had no idea why. Dad was no help: he just turned a blind eye. As I've said, we had plenty of contact with other children and it soon became painfully obvious that we led different lives from them: we were restricted in everything we did. What hurt most was not being different, but knowing we were different.

The house on Bucklow Avenue had three bedrooms but I insisted on sharing mine with Freda. By now I'd stopped being jealous of her and we clung together. It was the start of an intense relationship that has grown stronger every day. I am a rough sleeper and had nightmares as a child. Freda and I shared a bed and often I'd kick her out and she'd spend the night sleeping on the floor. Mother took to pinning her to the sheets! One night Mother insisted that we slept apart and put Freda in the third bedroom. She was only there one night because I went berserk. I couldn't stand being on my own and screamed the house down. Even when she was brought back into my room I was petrified of the dark. If I needed the toilet in the night I'd wake Freda and make her stumble out of the room and on to the landing ahead of me. She'd turn on the landing light while I stood outside my parents' bedroom door and shouted, making certain they were awake and knew I was going to the toilet. Afterwards I'd run back to bed, often leaving Freda sitting asleep on the stairs, and Mother would have to get up, turn the light out and carry Freda back to bed. I am still afraid of the dark: I wouldn't walk down a dark lane at night if you offered me a million pounds.

When I was nine, we moved from Bucklow Avenue to 301 Great Western Street in Rusholme and I started to attend Lloyd Street school where I excelled in composition. Long before I went to school Dad had taught me how to tell the time, spell and count. He cared about things like that although Mother didn't. It was at around this age that I really started to notice how Mother drove Dad. One incident from this period stands out in my memory. Mother wanted a coat so Dad saved up and they went into Manchester where she saw a full-length black seal fur. She demanded he bought it. Dad was horrified as it cost fourteen pounds and he only earned three pounds a week. Mother insisted she had it and threw a tantrum until he gave way. He was in debt for the next year paying for it. Her spending broke Dad. He had one suit hanging in the wardrobe, while she had rows of extravagant clothes. She was very fashion-conscious, always flicking through magazines to see what she should be wearing. She never had to buy hats, though: she was a clever needlewoman and used to buy blocks of felt from John Lewis and make beautiful ones.

Dad had loads of adventures on the police force. One day he came home with safety pins all down his legs, holding his trousers together. He told us that he'd come across a woman who had been drinking heavily and was on a bridge threatening to jump into the river Irwell. She was screaming that she was going to kill herself and took all her clothes off so she was absolutely starkers. The police used to wear capes so Dad flung his around her and she got hold of his trousers and ripped them off him. Left him standing there in his underpants! One of his least favourite jobs was mortuary duty, seeing to the bodies as they were brought in. Once a man had gassed himself and his body was rigid, curved round. It was Dad's job to wash it. He was doing his feet when a big wet hand came up and hit him in the neck. Dad was petrified, until he realized that the man's body was so curved that his hand had spun round out of control. Another time when a man's body came in Dad took off the clothes and put them on a table next to the slab. Then he went off to have a cup of tea. On his return he nearly had a heart attack because the man was sitting up on the slab putting his socks on. Apparently he'd had some sort of seizure and the coldness of the slab had brought him round.

Dad's best friend in the police force was a big Scotsman called Angus, who had grown up on the Bowes-Lyon estate. He'd played in the grounds with the then Duchess of York. When the Duke and Duchess came to inspect the Manchester police, my father couldn't believe it when she stopped by Angus, who was standing to attention next to him. She said, 'Surely it's not Angus?' and he said, 'Yes, Ma'am,' and she said, 'Fancy seeing you here, after all these years.' He had tears in his eyes, and my father said it was fantastic.

Six months after that a terrible thing happened. Angus and my father had swapped shifts, and during the night Angus got involved with a drunken man on the Irwell bridge. They'd fought and the man fell into the river. Angus jumped in after him and the man grabbed him by the neck and drowned him. Father was terribly upset: not only should it have been his shift but he knew he was the better swimmer and felt he could have survived the attack. It upset him so much that after Angus's death his attitude to policing changed. He didn't think it was worth it any more and he stopped putting so much effort into it. He sat exams and passed them but refused to become a sergeant, and later, when I was singing, the Chief Constable begged him to become an inspector but he wouldn't. Since the loss of his friend his heart hadn't been in it. However, he inspired our cousin, Albert Driver, who followed him into the force and finished up as Chief Superintendent of Leicester city police.

With Dad working such long hours, Freda and I were really brought up by Mother. She'd never wanted children and neglected us until she found I could sing. Then everything changed for me, if not for Freda. The potential Mother saw in me reminded her of the excitement she'd had in entertaining the troops. She was eager to taste show business again and her enthusiasm proved the kiss of death for my childhood.

CHAPTER THREE

Manchester's Latest Singing Sensation!

O n the Oxford Road, the wide thoroughfare that runs through the south of Manchester, from the city centre to Didsbury, there once stood a little old theatre that was the pride and joy of Manchester. It was situated opposite Platt Fields, near to where I was brought up, and was called the Leslie's Pavilion. It was a gorgeous one-floored theatre, built of wood and furnished with beautiful gold-pointed seats. All through the winter the management presented the hit summer-season shows from the end of piers in holiday resorts. Each show came for a fortnight to entertain us Mancunians. Like many people then, my parents shunned the picture houses, where talkies were beginning to make an impression, and never looked further than the local theatre. Occasionally, for a treat, Freda and I were taken along as well.

The summer-season folk were regulars at the Pavilion and each year a company called the Quaintesques, who were stationed in Rhyl, would arrive. They were a troupe of

18

men who dressed as women, and the star of the show was Billy Manders. He was a big man and impersonated the popular singer Sophie Tucker, wearing a wig, fabulous beaded gowns, and had a chiffon handkerchief hanging from a ring on his finger. Very stunning and theatrical. These drag shows were all the rage at the time and my parents had no qualms about taking little children to see them.

I can remember thinking that the people on stage looked beautiful in their sophisticated gowns and fabulous hairstyles. It didn't matter to me whether they were men or women. I was just enthralled. My parents were fans of the Quaintesques and whenever they appeared at the Pavilion Freda and I were guaranteed a night out in the cheap stall seats.

In the winter of 1928 I was seven and a half and, unknown to me, as we set off to see the Quaintesques that evening, my whole life was about to change. For some reason, goodness knows why, my parents had bought Freda and me little sets of sou'wester, macintosh and wellies all to match. Mine was red and Freda's was yellow. We wore these to the Pavilion that night and fancied ourselves so much in them that we refused to take them off. It was a hot night and we sweltered whilst we sat there, perched up on the back of our seats to get a better view of the stage. This show was going on and Billy Manders asked the audience to join in with a chorus. I got quite carried away, booming away in the back row, louder than everyone else.

At the end of the song, Billy peered into the audience and said, 'That was very, very good, but would that little lad that was singing please come forward on to the stage?' My mother pushed me out into the centre aisle of the theatre, with everyone turning round to look at me. I felt I should at least take my sou'wester off but I walked up on to the stage and joined Billy, saying, 'I'm not a little lad, I'm a little girl!' He laughed and said, 'Right, let's sing it again.' It was a dreadful song called 'Izzy Azzy Wozzy'. There we were, this giant of a man dressed in a sequined frock and me in my red macintosh and wellies. We brought the roof down and I was presented with a bottle of toffees – my first fee!

Whilst I enjoyed singing on the stage with Billy, in the audience my mother listened to the laughter and the applause and her mind went into overdrive. She had always wanted to be on the stage herself, but she had never really had the nerve. Here was her daughter going a step further than singing to the piano in the parlour and she decided there and then that I belonged on the stage. Suddenly she launched herself into good deeds and committees. My father couldn't understand where all this charity had appeared from, until he realized what she was doing. Being on committees enabled her to push me as a potential enter-tainer. She soon took charge of the entertainment committee at the new Co-operative Society shop on Platt Lane and decided to raise funds by throwing children's concerts. One was *The Wedding of the Painted Doll* in which I was given the plum role as the vicar. Poor Freda was cast as the bridesmaid, but soon gave up holding the bride's train to scamper round the back of me to cling on to the tails of my coat. She was terrified and cried all through the songs I had to sing. But I had the time of my life. I was so confident and eager to entertain. The audience paid threepence each – to see a group of petrified children unsure of what they were doing. The Leslie's Pavilion only charged a ha'penny to see the Quaintesques!

Having secured my appearances at the Co-op, Mother turned her attention further afield. Manchester had four huge parks at the time – Alexandra, Princess, Platt and Whitworth – and each had little huts or chalets on them where retired policemen used to go for a smoke, to play cards and dominoes. Mother identified these veterans as a captive audience and formed a committee to put on concerts for them. I was dragged along in my best dress and made to sing to these old chaps. The concerts were awful, featuring anyone Mother could persuade to go on. One time, in Platt Park, I was sitting in the front row, waiting to go on, and had a sore throat. Mother gave me half a lemon to suck, thinking it would heal my throat. It was very juicy and sour, and as I sat there sucking it loudly some poor man was on stage, trying to play his trumpet. He kept watching me, and couldn't help dribbling in sympathy. Eventually he had to stop playing and said, 'If you don't put that lemon away I'm going to choke.'

Then Mother started to take me to all the charity galas and talent contests around Manchester and the whole of the North-west. I won them all, hands down. My prizes were usually gold medals. For years this carried on, with me singing in little shows to whoever would pay to see them, then singing cute little numbers in the talent shows, and collecting my medal. My first important date was at the Victoria Theatre in Burnley. As I was made up by Mother in the dressing room, we could hear the most terrible noise going on outside the theatre. She went to investigate and found it was everybody passing the stage door in clogs on their way home from the mills. It sounded like armies of men marching.

When I was eleven, I was picked to take part in a big concert in aid of police welfare at the old Gaiety Theatre at the Manchester Hippodrome. It took place in the afternoon of Thursday 22 October 1931, and was my first large-scale public appearance. Mother knew it was an important concert for me and stayed up until three in the morning with my auntie Mabel finishing the dress I was to wear. With a top hat and a cane, I looked a picture. For the first time I didn't have Mother accompanying me on the piano: instead I had a full orchestra and I rose to the occasion, belting out my two numbers. It was called a 'Grand Variety Matinée' and my part was very small, but I shared the bill with real professionals, including Dame Sybil Thorndike who read poetry. Dame Sybil was the greatest actress of her generation who created the role of St Joan in the classic Bernard Shaw play, and she held this audience spellbound. Although she was not impressed at having to share a dressing room with a precocious eleven-year-old, she gave me the best advice I would ever receive: 'If you want to go into this business, there's one rule – don't ever be late.'

Dame Sybil was the first person I'd ever seen applying makeup. Soon afterwards I settled into my own makeup routine, which I followed for years. I used greasepaint, Leichner stick makeup, which many people in the business had boycotted during the First World War as it was considered too German. I used number five as a base, applied evenly with my fingers, then rouge, which was number nine, then dark grey eyeshadow. Then powder over all that.

I'd draw on faint eyebrows and then, in those days, lines right round my eyes to make them stand out. I also had a little stick of black grease, and a candle; I would light the candle, put a cocktail stick through the black and hold it over the candle to warm it, then drop it on to my eyelashes to make them darker and build them up. Then, finally, came lipstick.

Mother channelled all her energies into making me a successful performer and became very strict. She wouldn't let me do anything she deemed unsuitable: she banned tennis, swimming (it would make my bust too big), horse-riding (it would make my hips too big), dancing, anything that might lead to an injury and stop me working. She was always worried that cigarette smoke would affect my voice, and as in those days nearly everybody smoked it seemed I never went anywhere. Taking the advice of a theatre manager, she persuaded the Terence Byron Repertory Company to take me on for two seasons when I was ten. It was based at the King's Theatre, Longsight, and it was there that I learned how to project my voice and to go on stage without nerves. Whilst I was there we did plays and two pantomimes. I used to rehearse all morning, and go to school in the afternoon then go on stage at night. I starred in one of the plays, *Daddy-long-legs*, playing an adopted child. It was a wonderful experience, and made me realize that there was more to life than mimicking Gracie Fields as a singer.

A repertory company consists of a group of actors who work on a different play every week. You act in one for one week and rehearse another at the same time. Being part of a company like that taught me how to learn and retain lines. There were about fifteen of us in the company and I took all the children's roles. I was the only child in the company and sometimes had to play a boy – I got very butch. I had the summer off, before going back for the pantomime. I was a child prodigy and enjoyed it so much; I felt I could cope well with being a straight actress but my mother wanted me to sing. She felt the money was in the musical side so she pushed me into variety.

Mother signed me up with a manager and he enrolled me at a private school in High Street, Manchester. Its pupils were mainly sickly children who needed special attention, and my manager, whom I don't intend to dwell on, placed me there because he knew they'd turn a blind eye to me being taken away for performances and rehearsals. Whenever little Betty was needed to sing some-where, money would exchange hands between my manager and the headmaster. The school was eventually closed down.

With Mother pushing me so much my enthusiasm for singing disappeared. I'd enjoyed winning the talent shows and showing off on stage, but suddenly those days seemed past and the discipline of being a professional performer took over. Mother was so determined that I was going to succeed that she stripped me of my confidence: she criti-cized everything I did, telling me I was 'bloody useless' and making me believe I was an unattractive child who couldn't put a foot right without her guidance. Even though I had a manager, she wouldn't loosen her grip on me, and went round all the northern agents to get me dates in places like Burnley, Wigan, Stockport, Halifax and Rochdale. All that summer, when I wasn't in rep, she took me round the northern theatres and propelled me on to the stage to do my routine. The northern circuit was considered quite good, with great audiences. The mill people would visit on a Monday to gather new jokes to tell their friends.

The songs I sang were modern, popular songs, and I imitated Gracie Fields' hits like 'Sing As We Go', and 'The Biggest Aspidistra In The World', corny little numbers that I detested but Mother adored. I hated singing them and I hated being on the huge stage all by myself. I soon discovered that being in variety was the loneliest life in the world. Each week I'd go to a theatre and stand on that stage, on my own, for about fifteen minutes, singing. There was nobody to help me, and if I didn't get over to the audience within the first two minutes, I'd die a death. I used to say to my mother, 'If I can't be an actress, why can't I be in a show where we're with the same people all the time?' but she insisted on me touring around, getting experience by working with different people.

There were so many acts, so many faces illuminated by the stage lights. Most of them ignored me; as a child I just got in their way backstage. However, I wasn't the only juvenile on the bills at the time, and I soon made friends with two other little girls who I always seemed to be bumping into. Beryl Reid was about my age and we hit it off wonderfully. She had a comedy routine and was sweet on stage. She was the best mimic in the business. She'd bring the house down and, like mine, her mother would stand in the wings watching every move, every gesture, every facial expression. I didn't get to meet Tessie O'Shea often but when I did we'd run off to a dressing room and chatter away together like two old women rather than the children we were.

The reason our paths seldom crossed was because we were working in variety, and variety means just that. As Tessie and I were both juvenile singers we weren't often booked on the same bill, unless the manager had made a mistake. Once, Mother and I arrived to play Hull and she was mortified to discover that Tessie was on the same bill. Tessie was a little older than me but we were both vital, bubbly, modern singers. Tessie had the added attraction of accompanying herself on the banjulele, a cross between the banjo and the ukulele. When we arrived on the Monday morning and our two mothers met, the stage hands dived for cover as they set upon each other. Tessie and I hid in a dressing room and left them to it. We were good friends, although our mothers hated each other.

When I was booked at a theatre I had no idea who I would be sharing the bill with until I turned up, hoping that someone I knew was in the theatre. One particular act announced itself by smell, and I would always squeal with delight if I recognized it. They were a fabulously funny threesome called Wilson, Keppel and Betty, and I'm pleased to say we toured with them a lot. The smell came from a floral disinfectant they used. They always bought it from a Scottish firm and used gallons of it. Their act, 'Cleopatra's Nightmare', is as famous now as it was all those years ago and is much copied, but no one can capture their charm and originality. Wilson and Keppel were thin, tall men, who dressed in long white nightshirts and wore fezzes. Betty dressed as a veiled Cleopatra and the three would perform an outrageous Egyptian dance on sand. The sandalwood disinfectant was used to perfume the sand. I adored their act and as soon as the orchestra struck up their music, called 'Ballet Égyptien' I'd tear to the side of the stage and laugh myself silly watching them.

After leaving the Terence Byron Company, aged twelve, I toured with my first revue. It was called *Mixed Bathing*. Now, a touring revue was something very different from appearing haphazardly in northern theatres. The whole point of a touring revue is that it tours all over the country. Having signed me up on the tour, Mother said goodbye to Father, packed a case and that was the start of my life as a working artist, living out of a suitcase. Freda was nine and with Dad out policing all day Mother had no option but to bring her with us. We two little girls ran along railway platforms, dodging the steam from the engines, trying to keep up with our determined mother, striding purposefully ahead.

The revue toured all over England, Ireland, Scotland and Wales, appearing in all the number-one theatres. We travelled on Sundays, and on arriving in a new town the first thing we'd do was locate the boarding house Mother had booked us into. She'd have written ahead to the theatre's stage manager asking for a recommended billet and we'd arrive on the doorstep of each new place, clutching our bags and hoping the landlady was going to be kind. Inevitably it wasn't the landladies we had problems with, but the teachers at the schools we were sent to. Every Sunday night, Freda and I would cuddle up together and pray, 'Please God, make the teachers be kind to us.'

The next morning, Mother would drag us to the local school. Obviously we weren't in the same class because of the age difference, and Freda used to get terribly upset. I remember one school I went to whilst I was playing the

Sunderland Empire. Mother left us at the gates and all the children were staring at us. The headmaster got hold of me, put me on his knee and started to fondle me, saying, 'You're a nice little girl. How much money do you make at the theatre?' I said, 'I'm not telling you because I don't know how much money I make,' because my mother never told me. I had no idea at all. He was annoyed and made me stand on a chair in the middle of the hall then told all the children to march round me and stare at me. Dreadful man. I told my mother he'd been touching me, but it didn't bother her. I had an awful lot of that: men seemed to think that if you were on the stage you were used to it and I was still only twelve. It shocked me at first and I hated it, but in the end I had to get used to it.

Whilst I settled into that week's school, Mother enjoyed herself at the theatre, taking my band call. She'd hand out the music arrangements to the orchestra and listen whilst they rehearsed. I would be at school all day, go home for my tea, then get to the theatre for about half past five. There'd be two performances, at six and then at eight thirty. Thankfully there was a strict rule that children couldn't be inside the theatre at all after nine thirty, so I was always on early in the programme, normally finishing just before the interval. That was a good thing but I wish they'd been a bit more strict and stopped me going on altogether. From then on, my childhood was school and singing. No playing.

Travelling around like that was hard. Mother always rented two rooms: a bedroom for herself and a sitting room with a divan to act as our bed. She was an asthmatic and couldn't walk very far, so we never ventured out of the digs because she wouldn't let us out without her. Saturdays were our day off and we'd do a bit of shopping, but nothing more. She didn't think to take us girls to a film and discouraged us from associating with anybody of our own age. When we were shopping we often called in at 'guinea' shops, which sold cheap dresses, where she bought my stage outfits: lovely evening gowns bought for a guinea, which she altered to fit me.

Whenever I was in variety, apart from charity appearances, I always had my own dressing room. Because I spent so much time in it we'd make it as nice as we could. We used to get pretty material and hang it on loops from the hangers, where my clothes were supposed to go, then hang my clothes on top. At night, we lifted up the hem and folded it over to cover the clothes to keep them clean and the cleaners from knocking into them as they swept the floors. I used to make covers for the dressing-tables, with long frills and pockets to keep evening shoes and bits and pieces in. And I'd have a tray with all my makeup on, brush and comb and perfume.

Everything came down to routine. We'd arrive at the theatre, go straight to my dressing room where I'd get made up then sit with Freda and wait. There were no books, no toys, no games. We just waited for the call-boy to knock and say I was next on. I'd go on, do the act, come back, then sit in the dressing room for another two hours waiting for the next time to go on. Mother wouldn't sit with us – she'd be having a natter in another dressing room. Freda would read and I did needlework. We'd just sit there together and I think that's why we're still so close: as far as we're concerned, our minds are as one.

My stage act was dictated by Mother. I'd usually do four chirpy songs, then a little talk and lastly the impression of Gracie Fields. All the time I sang Mother stood at the side of the stage, beating the tempo. She liked the act always to be the same and would threaten me, 'If you do such and such an action, just wait until you come off!' Then I'd be on the stage and spontaneously do a natural action. When I came off – wham, another slap across the face. After a while stage managers refused to have her in the wings as she was such an upsetting influence. Sometimes Freda was allowed to take her place, and whenever I was frightened on the stage I'd look at her out of the corner of my eye, which made me feel better.

Ever restless and seeking new opportunities to have the name 'Betty Driver' recognized around the country, Mother's next step was to badger the BBC into booking me for broadcasts. I was engaged to appear on a variety programme called *Monday Night at Eight*. It was to be my first broadcast. I was working in Manchester at the time so Mother and I travelled down to London on the train. It was awful weather, blanket fog all the way, and the journey was slow. When we arrived we jumped into a taxi and sped to Broadcasting House. I was a quarter of an hour late for rehearsals and was terrified as I pushed the studio door open. The director stared at me and said, 'Who are you?' I smiled weakly and said, 'I'm Betty Driver from Manchester. I'm booked to sing "I'm On A Seesaw".' He turned his back on me and said, 'What time's the next train back to Manchester? Well, whenever it is you and your mother had better get on it. You are a quarter of an hour late and I don't tolerate that.' So Sybil Thorndyke's advice had been right. We went home, and from that moment on I have never been late for anything. It was a humiliating experience.

Thankfully the BBC didn't give up on me and I was soon back at Broadcasting House. Radio became part of my life, and a very enjoyable part too. Whenever I was available I'd be called into Langham Place to record a song or two, or a little playlet, to put out whenever there were gaps in the schedule. Just cheerful little numbers. If I was singing, I'd be placed right up close to the microphone and the band would be up at the other end of the room so they didn't drown my voice. Mother would sit in the booth with the director, making certain I didn't improvise and stuck to my routine. Even with her beady eye on me it was still better than singing on stage.

Although my time with the BBC was mainly spent in singing, it was the occasional acting that I looked forward to. Standing around a microphone with a group of actors, most much older than me, watching their facial expressions change as they became their characters. Wonderful. I was fascinated by the man with the sound effects. He used to stand very close to me and create wonderful noises – coconut shells for horses' hoofs, thunder sheets and walking in sand or gravel trays. If the script said I was drinking I never held the cup, it was all down to sound effects. The boy poured water close to the microphone, then I took a sip and swallowed. I had to be careful not to turn the pages of my script or music close to the microphone. The recordings were done during the day as each evening I was on stage in *Mixed Bathing*.

I was in *Mixed Bathing* for two years. Two years of travelling every Sunday, spending six days in digs, five days at a new school each week and shows in the evenings. Eventually the authorities caught up with my mother and insisted that Freda have some proper schooling. She was nearly eleven and the decision was made to send her back to Manchester to live with Father in Rusholme. Mother's parents and her sister Winifred moved in to look after them and straight away started to persecute Freda. Aunt Winifred had always been regarded as the rose of the family, but by this time she was wilting and she was jealous of the eleven-year-old beauty who was starting to bloom. She poisoned my grandmother's mind against Freda and they starved and neglected her, locking her out of the house. The same people who indulged me and thought I was wonderful, had no time for Freda at all. Dad was working all the time and had no idea of what was going on behind his back. Or if he did he turned a blind eye.

It was so bad that the headmistress had to call on Dad and threaten him with the authorities if he didn't buy Freda a new pair of shoes. He hadn't noticed the huge holes in her only pair and that Grandmother hadn't bothered to buy new ones. I used to send Freda my cast-off costumes and she managed to keep some for herself, although anything decent was snatched up by Winifred. I once sent a pair of silver stage shoes and Freda was so desperate that she stuffed them with paper and painted them black to wear to school – high-heeled theatrical shoes! Meanwhile, I carried on singing, but without the comfort of seeing Freda's cheerful face when I returned to the dressing room after performing.

I felt like the loneliest girl in the world and there seemed no hope of life ever changing. But my big break was just around the corner.

CHAPTER FOUR

Great Britain's Youngest Leading Lady

In 1934 I was fourteen and had been a professional enter-tainer for two years already. I'd toured the country in a top-ranking revue, been part of a respected repertory company and was making a name for myself in radio. Another child might have been happy with her lot, but I wasn't. Freda was still in Manchester, getting the schooling I was missing out on, and I hated my lonely life. And even though everything so far had happened at her instigation, Mother wasn't happy either. My career wasn't reaching the heights she had expected and she decided that this was because I wasn't playing the big, number-one theatres in London. The main theatre groups had their head offices in London and they controlled bookings at prestige venues like the Palace in Manchester, the Hippodrome in Birmingham, the King's in Glasgow and the Empire in Leeds, so it was almost impossible for northern artists to play London, or get very far, without a London agent. The best agents would track down provincial talent and bring them to London then spread out to the main variety halls. In the thirties each city had five or six theatres and, by and large, it is now only the number-one venues that are still standing. On a rare visit to Dad in Manchester, Mother took his five pounds' savings and bundled me off to the bright lights of the capital. Dad was horrified and warned me against London: it was a very wild city, he said.

Mother's plan was to walk around the theatres and see what happened. We found reasonable lodgings in Brixton and took the tram into the West End on our first morning. Standing in Shaftesbury Avenue, in the middle of the theatre district, Mother looked up and down then announced we'd try the Windmill, a big vaudeville theatre located on Great Windmill Street, built originally as a cinema. It had only been converted into a theatre in 1931.

I'll say something for my mother, she certainly had guts and determination. She marched straight into the theatre and demanded that the manager audition me. He looked me up and down and, to my amazement, agreed. Now, the Windmill did five shows a day and they weren't the sort of shows I was used to. During the Second World War, it became famous as the theatre that never closed, but even before then it was infamous for its nude acts. I had no idea and I don't think Mother did either. I had to audition in the interval between two shows; the audience was full of dirty old men.

The manager positioned a microphone on the stage then sat down with Mother and I wandered on nervously. I started to sing and I noticed, in the wings, all the nudes. Naked men were staring at me. I was shocked: I'd never seen a body before and I thought it was very rude, so I refused to carry on. I picked up my things and ran out of the theatre. I didn't stop until I was at the other end of Shaftesbury Avenue. Mother finally caught up with me and was furious. I said to her, 'I don't care what I do, I'm not going to work in that place!' I think she must have been as upset as I was because she didn't force me to return.

Instead, we walked through Leicester Square and we came across the Prince of Wales theatre. It looked respectable, so Mother went in and, once again, asked for the manager. He auditioned me there and then, on the spot. I sang a couple of numbers for him, mimicked Gracie Fields and he signed me up straight away, for five shows a day.

I arrived at the theatre for my first performance, very full of myself and expecting my own dressing room, but was soon brought down to earth when I was shoved in with the chorus. They cleared a space on the long communal dressing-table and left me to it. Like the Windmill, the Prince of Wales also had nudes but they were a more tasteful bunch. All the chorus worked as nudes, boys and girls, aged between sixteen and nineteen. There I'd be, getting ready with my mother, upstairs at the back of the theatre, sitting at a tiny corner of dressing-table, trying hard not to look at the rest of them. The law required all nude acts to stand perfectly still on the stage. The thing that got to me about working at the Prince of Wales were the dirty old men who sat in the theatre all day, through all five performances. Each show they moved forward a row until in the end they'd be sitting on the front row with their raincoats over their laps. The nudes were formed up into Greek and Roman tableaux. The boys wore very small jockstraps, skin coloured, and the girls had tiny pieces of tape covering them so they weren't completely starkers. They were all very good-looking and had marvellous bodies.

At first I didn't think I'd be able to cope with five shows daily but in fact it all went well. To help me remember how many times I'd been on Mother pinned a chart on the wall and chalked off each performance. The audience was mainly there to ogle the nudes but thankfully they liked me because I was a child and Mother still insisted that I wore little skirts. I certainly went down better than the comedians, who weren't female and kept their clothes on! I was there for two weeks, getting older each day, and the money wasn't good, so Mother's feet were soon itching and she started to look round for my next venue.

These theatres really acted as shop windows for new artists to show what they could do, and in the second week I was told there was a big agent in the theatre. I went on and did my spot and the next day he phoned and asked me to go and see him. His name was Bert Aza and he was in partnership with his brother, Archie Pitt, Gracie Fields' husband. Archie was the oldest of four brothers – Archie, Bert, Pat and Edgar – and he'd been the first to go into show business. Bert had taken his name from a cloth merchant, Aza, who when he and his brothers formed a tumbling act, had provided lengths of material for their stage costumes.

Mother was thrilled, convinced that fame was just around the corner. We went to his office in Charing Cross Road and he told me he wanted to book me for a revival of *Mr Tower of London*, which Gracie Fields had made famous nineteen years before. She had been just sixteen when she met

Archie, and she married him nine years later. I assumed I'd be playing one of the minor parts but Archie and Bert said they wanted me as the lead. Mother pointed out that I was only fourteen but they said that didn't matter; they were confident I could easily carry it off. It had been Gracie's part, and I left the office overwhelmed by the prospect of stepping into her shoes. Mother signed two contracts that day: one for me to join the revue, and the other with Bert Aza, agreeing that he would be my exclusive agent. From that day, sixty-six years ago, the Azas have been my agents, first Bert and when he died his gorgeous wife Lillian took over.

Bert and Lillian had a son, Morris, who was the same age as Freda, and I was more or less brought up with him. I remember the first time we met: I was seventeen or so and his parents were throwing a party where we all entertained each other. I was a little in awe of the guests, like Stanley Holloway, because I didn't see myself as a star. Yet there was a real family atmosphere and that's one of the reasons I liked the Azas so much. While I was relaxing, Mother would be working the room for contacts to further my career.

When Lillian died in 1984, I was distraught and felt I couldn't go on without her support, but wonderful Morris took over the agency. I adore him and look upon him as a brother and his wife, Sheila, as a sister. Now, when people say, 'Why have you got an agent? What use is an agent to you?' I say, 'He's a lot of use. Firstly he's my dearest friend and secondly he's a brilliant contract reader. He cares to read the small print, which I would gloss over.' I pay my agent 10 per cent every week gladly. Without the support of Morris and his family I would have retired years ago. The family have always been a joy to work with – and I knew they wouldn't hit me if something went wrong! We'd often see in the New Year at the Aza family house, and although I don't remember ever having a cuddle from Mother I would receive a kiss on New Year's Eve. A peck on the cheek and that was it for the next twelve months. The lack of affection never bothered me though, as I didn't know any better.

Before I started in *Mr Tower of London* I was booked for an engagement in Manchester, at the Palace Theatre. It was a wonderful booking and I belted out my numbers with gusto. One night, at the end of the performance, George Formby came backstage to see me with his wife Beryl. George was quiet and Beryl did all the talking. She said they'd enjoyed my performance and asked if I'd appear in a film that George was making for Butcher's Films called *Boots! Boots!.* I'd known George from variety where he was top of the bill and had a fabulous act, and Freda and I had often seen him on Pathé newsreels, which would feature snippets of his jokey songs and chirpy greetings. Off-stage he was gormless but very sweet. Beryl was made in the same mould as Mother and drove him completely. There was a spot in the film where George was to visit a nightclub and they wanted me to be the cabaret singer. I was to have a song then do a sketch with George. Mother was all for it so shortly after-wards I found myself in a tiny little film studio called the Albany, situated above a garage off Regent Street.

It was my first experience of film and I was apprehensive. I was given my own dressing room, in which I found, laid out on a chair, the most beautiful gold dress I was to wear in my scene. George was a lovely chap but very slow-witted and I soon realized that Beryl had to push him because otherwise he'd have just sat about happily doing nothing all day. It was a low-budget film, costing just £3,000, and was being made quickly so there wasn't much time to panic. There was no real plot, just a series of scenes set around George as a hotel boots, doing comedy routines with the hotel staff. Beryl played the dancing scullery maid and she and George ended up performing together in the hotel cabaret.

The director rehearsed the cabaret scene quickly. I wore the dress and wandered around the tables being very sophisticated and alluring, singing my number. The rehearsal went well. Too well, in fact, because as soon as I'd finished Beryl said, 'George, she's not singing that, it's the best number in the film.' George said, 'But she must do it, it's been written for her.' She said, 'I'll do that number!' and she had her way. All this was said very loudly in front of me. I was broken-hearted. George tried to cheer me up, saying, 'Never mind, we've still got our sketch together.'

In the sketch I was to be a maid, and he was the boots. But after we'd rehearsed it the same thing happened. Beryl watched us enjoying the scene then stormed on to the set and pointed at me, shouting, 'George! That kid. She's not going on in this film. I'm not having a kid outshining me!' Mother and I were bundled on to the next train out of town. The producers felt bad about the way I'd been treated and refused to take my name off the credits. Every now and again the film is shown on television, normally in the early hours of the morning, and my name rolls up with the credits even though I don't appear in it at all!

Thankfully I was able to forget about my run-in with the Formbys when I started on *Mr Tower of London*. It was to be a touring revue, playing all the number-one theatres. Archie

Pitt directed and my leading man was Norman Evans, a relatively unknown comic in his mid-thirties. It was a fabulous revue, made up of sketches, solo singing from me and comedy from Norman. The setting was a tour around London and there were scenes set in popular places, like Madame Tussaud's, the Tower and on the top of a double-decker bus. Gracie Fields had toured with it for nine years from 1918. In her day the revue had been made up of members of her and Archie's families. This time round we had a marvellous chorus of twelve girls, and I immediately made friends with them.

After rehearsing for two weeks, we opened at the Palace Theatre, Southampton, then began to tour around the country. Archie Pitt was the first person to ignore Mother and deal directly with me. During rehearsals Mother had tried to make her presence felt but he had handled her wonderfully, giving her the impression that he was taking in all her ideas but then, to my relief, ignoring them. He treated me like a young lady and drew out the best from me. In return I always gave the best performance I could so I wouldn't disappoint him.

The show ended with me singing a solo. Then the curtain fell, everyone applauded and Norman joined me on stage to take our curtain call. After the first performance, during the applause Archie, who knew I loved animals, came on to the stage and handed me a huge bouquet of pink roses. In the middle was a puppy, a beautiful little Pekinese. Well, it was the most wonderful moment of my life. This little sable and white puppy looking up at me. The audience went wild, I cried, Norman flushed with envy and Mother gritted her teeth, knowing she'd have to let me keep the dog after

Archie had made such a performance of giving her to me. I called her Julie and she lived to be fourteen. Archie had bred her from his own sleeve Pekes and had given another from the same litter to Mrs Simpson, just before she became the Duchess of Windsor. They were called sleeve Pekes because Oriental ladies carried them in the sleeves of their kimonos.

Norman Evans was my first leading man, and I couldn't have asked for a better one. Looking back, he must have thought I was terribly precocious. There he was, aged thirty-five, having been in the business for years without much recognition and there was me, fourteen, landing a plum part. He was also handled by Aza Management and became one of my closest friends. He had a wicked sense of humour, though, and used to play terrible practical jokes on me. One day he got very cross with me because I was being obnoxious about something. Just before I went on to do a sketch, he smudged my makeup and I had to walk on-stage with black stripes down my cheeks. I was so thrilled for him when, shortly after the revue finished, he achieved the fame he deserved. He created a wonderful character – one of variety's all-time classics: Fanny Fairbottoms. He'd wear a frightful red wig with a headscarf and stand on stage behind a brick wall and gossip to an invisible neighbour. The sketch was called 'Over The Garden Wall' and made him a household name. Years later Les Dawson resurrected the idea for his Cissie and Ada sketches with Roy Barraclough, who worked alongside me later at the Rovers as Alec Gilroy.

I had a great time in the show and adored the family atmosphere amongst the cast. I was sharing the top of the bill with Norman but we were encouraged not to act it up as stars. I went round with the chorus girls, having a laugh. At the end of the show, before the finale, I did my singing act. Bert's wife, Lillian, insisted that I looked stunning for these numbers and had a dress brought over from Paris for me. It was a beautiful blue and skin-tight, and I wore a white fox-fur cloak over my shoulders. About a month after we opened a new conductor called Atti Baker joined us. He was a marvellous man: he even knew if I was breathing in the wrong place and would alter the music to suit me. Back then, in 1934, stages were covered in dark brown linoleum, which was polished because a wooden stage was full of splinters and dust. To make my entrance I had to walk through an archway and down three little steps towards the footlights. My mother used to stand in the wings and say, 'Mind the step.' One day, I walked on in my posh frock to my music, started down the steps, looking all gorgeous and caught my toe on the top one, fell on my stomach and slid right to the front of the footlights. I ended up looking right at the orchestra. I just lay there and said, 'Hello, Atti,' then got up and did the act with Mansion polish all over my dress, from my bust to my knees. As luck would have it, the reporters were in and the next day there were all these write-ups in the papers saying, 'The most unusual entrance ever seen in the theatre, from Betty Driver'.

At around this time someone asked Mother if I wanted to make a record. Of course, she thought this was a wonderful idea. I didn't think it was a big deal but I recorded it at Abbey Road. To coincide with King George V's silver jubilee celebrations the song was called 'Jubilee Baby'. I didn't hear the results until almost fifty years later when a fan found a copy on a second-hand record stall and sent it

to me. I was thrilled – even though I sounded like a stran-
gled earwig! It was eighteen keys too high – but it was a
bright little number.

When I had been in *Mr Tower of London* for about two years,
we played in Poplar in the East End. I was sixteen now and
I loved playing to East End audiences as they were so appreciative. One night, Norman got very excited and full of
himself because C. B. Cochran was coming to see him. Sir
Charles Cochran was a well-known impresario, who put on
glamorous shows in the West End and had made stars of
Jessie Matthews and Anna Neagle. He had virtually invented
revue before the First World War, and mixed everything
from performing fleas and midget shows to the Russian
Ballet and classical actresses like Sarah Bernhardt. He had
also formed a partnership with Noël Coward and put on
glittering shows such as *Private Lives, Cavalcade* and *Bitter
Sweet.* By the time I met him he was in his sixties and
suffering from arthritis in the hip. He had a terrible limp
and leaned on a stick to stay upright. The only thing that
really helped the pain was hot baths and, sadly, that's how
he met his end: scalded to death in the tub. Anyway, we went
on and there was Cochran in the side box and Norman went
way over the top, winking at him, ignoring the rest of the
audience, delivering all his lines to the box.

The next day I was amazed to receive a phone call inviting
me to go to Cochran's office. I said they must have got it
wrong because he'd been to see Norman but was told that I
was the one he'd been impressed with. So I went to see him.
He said, 'How would you like to come into the West End, the
Adelphi Theatre? I'm putting on a big show, called *Home and*

Beauty, and I want you in it.' I was thrilled and stunned. Here was the most important man in theatrical revue and he was offering me a part in one of his shows. I'd been in the business long enough to know that this meant I was made.

I left Archie and the gang on *Mr Tower* with their congratulations ringing in my ear and Norman feeling overlooked. All the papers were speculating about Cochran's new revue. It had been written to celebrate the coronation of Edward VIII, but he abdicated to marry Mrs Simpson in the first week of our rehearsals. Cochran quickly rewrote a couple of scenes so we were now to celebrate the coronation of King George VI and Queen Elizabeth, which would take place in May 1937. The revue was a modern piece, written by A. P. Herbert and was set around a weekend house party at the ancestral home of the Earl and Countess of Mulberry. It was all about class and manners, and starred Binnie Hale as an American film star, Rose Mellow, and Gitta Alpar as Julika Kadar, a Hungarian prima donna. Gitta had started her career as a coloratura soprano in opera at Budapest. I had a couple of small roles, as a maid and as a house-guest, and was given a couple of solo numbers. One was especially written for me, 'A Nice Cup Of Tea', and became a popular song.

We rehearsed in Manchester for two weeks before opening in the Opera House on 23 December 1936. Mother booked tickets for the family to watch my opening night and hear me singing in a real top-line show. Unfortunately they never heard me sing on that stage, at least not in the revue.

When I arrived for the first rehearsals I was confronted with the chorus, who were known as the Cochran Young Ladies. They weren't real chorus girls because they never danced, just posed. They were all either titled, millionaires or whores. You've never seen such beautiful girls in your life. They arrived in mink coats and diamonds. Their fathers bought them places in the show and that's how Cochran always managed such lavish productions. One girl was an American who flew in every week in her own plane! I was still only sixteen and Mother kept all my money, so I'd look longingly at these beautiful girls and their fabulous clothes. After each show they'd all be met at the stage door by chauffeur-driven cars. They'd be in white mink to the floor or sable capes, and old men would meet them with flowers and jewels. The only person who met me was my mother.

Binnie Hale was a huge star and she terrified me. She was a large woman with a strident, booming voice, who reminded me of my mother. She was the star of the original production of the musical *No No Nanette* and had been the first person to sing 'Spread A Little Happiness'. We didn't get along at all and she was cruel to me. The first time Cochran rehearsed my song 'A Nice Cup Of Tea' I enjoyed it and it went down well with the company. Too well, in fact. Binnie was also in the sketch, which was set in the kitchen of this huge house and we were all playing the servants. When I'd finished, she said, 'I don't think that song suits you,' but I felt it was perfect and said so. She looked at me as if I were dirt, called Cochran over and told him she wanted to do the song. Of course, she was the big star and he had to give it to her. It was Beryl Formby all over again but much worse: the film had been just one day, but I'd been signed up to play in the revue for ten months and knew I'd have to sit in the scene whilst my song was sung by someone else. I was very upset but I still had another song. It was the final song of the whole revue, a wonderful scene

46

in which the women wore pink satin, furs and jewels, all designed by Norman Hartnell. In the middle of the scene I was to come on-stage, between two white pianos played by the famous pianists, Rawicz and Landauer, and sing a comedy song in the style of Gracie Fields. Of course, the inevitable happened. I performed the number in the rehearsal and loved it. But Binnie heard it in the dress rehearsal. After the curtain came down, she shouted, 'Cocky!' He came down to the stalls and she said, 'If that bloody kid goes on, I'm off! She's not doing that song in my show!' So I stood there in tears and my song was taken from me again.

After playing in a few number-one theatres, the revue was moved to the West End and we played the Adelphi in the Strand for ten months. Everyone in the revue hated everyone else, which was a shock for me, coming from the happy ensemble of *Mr Tower of London*. They constantly tried to put each other down. It was normal practice in those days for companies to understudy each other, and Cochran had asked me to understudy Binnie, saying that I worked like she did. So that the understudies knew what was expected of them, Cochran called a special rehearsal where we took the lead parts. Binnie Hale's part was me to a T. We did the whole show and it was fantastic. Then, from the back of the stalls, came this figure in furs, Binnie Hale. She walked down to the stage and said, 'Cocky, I've been watching the whole rehearsal and I'm telling you now, if I have to work on a stretcher, that cow will never go on!' And I never did! It nearly killed her. She had two carbuncles, one on each temple and had special wigs made to cover them. They made her ill and, after a while, just before each performance I would be asked to put on my understudy clothes because the doctor kept telling her she couldn't carry on. I'd get all excited, the music would start up then she'd appear and barge past me, saying, 'Out of my way!' And she'd go on, in agony, just to spite me. Then, after every performance, she'd pass out. It was stupid, really. She was a very fine artist, and needn't have been like that to me. She was a great performer, a big star, and I was just starting out. I'd been booked for this wonderful revue but I ended up as Binnie's understudy.

Binnie wasn't the only star jealous of me. I only ever spoke to Gracie Fields once, but she left me in no doubt as to what she thought of me, the child who'd taken on her revue and successfully made a name for myself. My agent, Lillian, asked me to call at the Azas' magnificent house in Maida Vale. It was huge and the housekeeper showed me into the drawing room. A woman was in there, wearing a plastic raincoat and a headscarf with a pair of black horn-rimmed glasses on her nose. We nodded to each other and said, 'Morning.' After a while Lillian came in and asked if I'd met Gracie. I said, 'No, I've never had the pleasure.' She looked me up and down and said, 'Likewise,' very cuttingly. Then she turned her back. And that was my meeting with Gracie Fields.

Back in Manchester, Freda was still having a terrible time. Eventually the headmistress at her school realized how badly neglected she was and arranged with the education committee for her to finish her schooling earlier than she should have. As she wasn't at school she was able to join us in London and moved into the flat we were renting in Parsons Green. Mother wasn't pleased to have her with us, but I was delighted. Since she'd been sent away to Manchester nearly three years previously, we'd seen each other about once a month, whenever I was playing at a theatre close enough to go home for a few hours. I'd spent all my spare time making dresses for dolls, which I'd sent her, and I'd written pages and pages of letters to her. Now I thought my lonely times at the theatre would cease but Mother was determined to keep us apart as much as possible. She would take me to the theatre every day at eleven o'clock in the morning, and leave Freda alone in the flat. Cochran never allowed people backstage so Mother would drop me off and come back for me later on after the performance, around eleven at night. I always thought she went back to the flat but she didn't, ever. Freda would be left alone for twelve hours and Mother was goodness knows where, spending the money I was earning.

For years Mother had stood guard over my virtue in theatres, seeing off the attentions of amorous comics and theatre managers. Now that I was sixteen I was receiving even more attention from the male members of the company but Mother wasn't around to look after me and I had more freedom. I was terribly naïve, even though I'd spent nearly five years in the theatre, but Mother had given me a talk about sex, which had terrified me. I'd been twelve and she'd gone into graphic detail, which left me fearing men. During the run of *Home and Beauty*, I was fortunate enough to meet a lovely actor called Leslie French, who took me under his wing, guiding me away from the society tarts of the chorus, saying, 'You're not that kind of girl, Betty. Do be careful.' In the show, Gitta Alpar, one of the stars, had a magnificent scene with two balalaika players, one of whom was called the Bull. A huge fella of six foot four, he took a fancy to me. He used to chase me all over the theatre. One week, we'd done a matinée and Mother met me at the stage door to take me to tea but I'd left my bag in the dressing room and had to go back. By this time, all the theatre lights had been turned off but I knew where my bag was so I wasn't bothered.

I entered my dressing room and groped around for the table. Then I heard somebody shuffle in behind. I froze. Suddenly this huge man grabbed me, and started to maul me, trying to kiss me. I thought he was going to rape me but I kept my head. With Dad being in the police force, he knew a lot about self-defence and had taught me how to take care of myself. Whilst this bloke was ripping at my clothes, I was trying to remember what to do. He turned me round to face him – and it clicked. I brought my knee up hard and he hit the floor like a stone. I thought I'd killed him! I flew out of the room screaming, 'I've killed the balalaika player because he was being rude!' Everyone thought it was so funny. After that the poor chap never spoke to me again.

In the winter of 1937 *Home and Beauty* came to the end of its run and I bade Binnie Hale a hearty goodbye. Mother was hoping I'd be able to make more recordings but the Azas had been busy on my account. On leaving the Adelphi I travelled to Brighton where I was booked to perform on the Palace Pier in Jimmy Hunter's *Brighton Follies*, a famous upmarket company. After the stress of working with Binnie and Gitta, it was a relief to be back on-stage doing my own routine. One night Basil Dean came to see the show. He was a big-time film producer and after the show he told me he had plans to turn me into a film star. I remembered my run-in with Beryl Formby, and whilst Mother dreamed of a career for me in Hollywood I wondered what this 'great, new experience' would mean to me.

CHAPTER FIVE

The Film Star

In 1938 Olivia de Havilland made *The Adventures of Robin Hood* for Warner Brothers, Vivien Leigh started work on *Gone With The Wind* for MGM, Ginger Rogers danced through *Carefree* at RKO and at ATP Studios in Ealing I starred in *Penny Paradise*. ATP was run by Basil Dean and turned out black and white comedies. It was one of the last films made by the company, and Basil was already making plans to give up film-making and return to his first love, the theatre. He was a hard-driving autocrat who had been a pioneer of troop entertainment during the First World War. He had already made a film star of Gracie Fields and signed up George Formby after seeing him in *Boots! Boots!* He oversaw the production of *Penny Paradise* and it was his idea to have me written into the plot. He wanted to launch one last British star and I was the chosen one. He signed me up to a five-picture deal and to make certain everyone working on the film was aware of my status, he insisted that my character was called 'Betty', in the same way that Gracie Fields always played 'Gracie' and George Formby 'George'. I was embarrassed by all the attention and was thankful that the rest of the cast didn't resent me.

There were three stars in the film, Edmund Gwenn, a gentle character actor who later won an Oscar for his portrayal of Father Christmas in the classic *Miracle on 34th Street*, Jimmy O'Dea, Ireland's top comedian, and me. The plot was straightforward, like many contemporary musical comedies. Tugboat skipper Joe Hibbert (Edmund) celebrated a win on the football pools but his crew of one, Pat (Jimmy) discovered he hadn't posted the coupon. I played Joe's daughter, who worked as a barmaid at the Casino public house, singing two chirpy numbers there, 'Stick Out Your Chin' and 'You Can't Have Your Cake'. Pat was in love with me but I agreed to marry the local dandy – obviously a villain as he drove a sports car and wore a permanent sneer.

Altogether I sang four songs in the film, always out of the blue – I seemed somehow to be near a piano when there was a poignant or emotional scene to be played!

When Joe finds out he hasn't won a fortune he fears he'll no longer be made skipper of the prestigious new tug he's been offered. I save the day, after seeing through my cad of a boyfriend and tricking the owner of the fleet into saying publicly that Joe can still skipper the new tug even though he hadn't won the pools.

During the filming of *Penny Paradise* I lived in Wimbledon Park with Mother and Freda. Mother took on the house with my money, and it was near the tennis courts in a lovely residential area. The house was only meant to be a temporary haven but we ended up renting it for three years, using it as a base whenever we were in London. As my working hours were long and unsociable, Mother couldn't leave

Freda at home and the three of us would go to the studios together. I was given a suite of rooms at Ealing, a dressing room, a lounge and *en suite* bathroom. It was like a flatlet, set in a row with others by the lawn at Ealing. Each film had its own flatlets for the leading artists. We worked long hours, receiving our schedules the night before. I had to have my hair washed and set at seven to be on the set for eight thirty, and it was hard work. There was rehearsal after rehearsal, and only a few scenes were recorded each day.

Carol Reed was the director, and went on to make classics such as *Our Man in Havana* and *The Third Man*. He knew I'd be nervous so had arranged for me to visit the studio the week before filming started to get accustomed to the place. During that week he read through my part with me and taught me different things. He told me that it was tradition to film the last shot first, which confused me. The last scene was me on a boat with the actor playing my father, singing whilst it swayed along. It took for ever to do that scene. It was shot in studio, with the boat set on rollers, lurching from side to side, against a back projector showing the sea. This was my first experience of film, and I'm not a good sailor. I went green.

I find filming relaxing, once I have got over the initial nerves. Sometimes it's too relaxing: it takes such a long time to light each shot and reposition the camera. I didn't socialize at night, just stayed at home learning my lines with Freda so I was word-perfect the next day for recording. Like my dad, I enjoyed being told what to do and working from schedules. I still do, and love the discipline of television, of having to be in the right place at the right time, knowing my lines and moves. I work well that way.

In those days, film singing all had to be dubbed. It was a long process which began with the artist making a record of the song. When the scene was filmed, the artist mimed along to the record. I found this difficult because I'm not the kind of person who does the same thing twice and inclinations would go wrong. In the film there'd be a mock band pretending to play behind me, mute, and I'd have to act all chirpy and jovial in front of the camera whilst trying to open and close my mouth in time to the record. It was a terrible way of going about it and I needed plenty of rehearsals. In the end I got quite good at it.

There was another film being shot at Ealing at that time, starring George Formby. His suite of dressing rooms was on the other side of the studio to mine but we kept bumping into each other, and my path was always crossing Beryl Formby's. If she remembered cutting me out of *Boots! Boots!* she never mentioned it, and acted as if nothing had happened. She took a shine to Freda, and when she couldn't be around she asked Freda to spy on George for her to make certain he was eating the right food. She'd put him on a strict diet and he wasn't allowed any of the food he longed for, just healthy, plain fare. It became Freda's job to follow him into the canteen and boss him into eating salads.

During the making of the film, I turned eighteen and the studio's publicity department made a tremendous fuss, throwing a lavish party for me. My dressing room was filled with flowers and even Mother got in on the act: she gave me a little white Hillman car with red leather inside. Of course, it wasn't really a present because I'd earned the money to pay for it but I loved it. I couldn't drive at that stage, so until I could learn a chauffeur was hired to drive me about in it.

George Formby was jealous of my Hillman and swapped his black Cadillac for a white Packard, to go one better. Then he tried to pinch my chauffeur, Dougherty, until I put my foot down. I found him lying on his back, in the uniform I had supplied, mending George's car, and warned George off.

Years later Beryl Formby sought me out after a variety show and told me she'd always admired my work. She told me about her life with George and how he was so very naïve and how she'd had to be so strong because people were forever trying to take advantage of him. She said, 'There was me, your mother and Kitty McShane and we were the most hated women in the business, although I think your mother beat me. Everyone hated the way she browbeat you girls.'

In all *Penny Paradise* was a good experience. Apart from my four musical numbers, I had plenty of acting to get my teeth into and I was fortunate to work with the best, on and off screen. The director, Carol Reed, the associate producer Basil Dearden, and head cameraman Ronald Neame, all became famous and all three were knighted in later life.

As far as my mother was concerned, from a young age my name had been Betty 'Bloody Fool' Driver and Freda was 'Streak of Lightning'. Every time I opened my mouth to offer an opinion on something she'd say, 'Shut up, you bloody fool.' That sort of thing goes with you through life and I expected everyone to treat me the same way. When I began work on the picture I had no self-confidence but these talented men worked on me, drawing me out of myself. Basil Dearden was especially kind and took pity on Freda too, who'd sit quietly watching every scene as it was rehearsed and filmed. There was a sequence in the film where titles had to roll over a shot of hands opening football pools coupons and Freda was asked if her hands could be used. Basil was always hanging around her, admiring her beautiful nails and asking to brush her hair, and he was determined to immortalize her hands! She didn't get a credit for it, mind.

As I said earlier, Norman Evans was a great friend but I'll never forget one day when he caused me deep embarrassment. I had a day's break in the filming of *Penny Paradise* and was planning to sit around the house with Freda, Mother having gone shopping in the West End. My plans were changed by the arrival at our front door of Norman and his wife, Annie, who invited us out for a ride. He had driven up in a great big white Cadillac and jumped out dressed in emerald-green plus fours, dark-red socks and tan shoes. His cap was in a different shade of green, he wore an apricot-coloured shirt, a red tie and an overcoat on top of the suit. He looked just like a marrow, gone off. The suit was for sports but the coat was a formal herring-bone affair, tailed. He looked ridiculous.

In those days fashion ruled my life and I said I wouldn't be seen dead with him. Freda agreed with me – she was as horrified as I was. However, Annie talked us into going on the trip, saying we wouldn't have to get out of the car and be seen with him. He took us to Windsor Great Park and it was a gorgeous day. He pulled up and said, 'I think we'll have some ice cream,' but I said, 'I am not getting out.' He went off and bought four huge cornets. On his way back he paused to admire some swans on the river and they attacked him because they were nesting. The ice cream went all over him. We sat in the car with what was left and he said I was rotten for not getting out. He had no idea that everyone in the park was laughing at him, and couldn't understand why Freda and I prided ourselves so much on our good taste.

Penny Paradise took four weeks to make, and shortly after completing it Basil left the company to return to the theatre. The film premièred in London and Manchester and on both occasions I was shoved into the background by Mother, who claimed the bouquets for herself and posed for photographs as if she were the star! Oddly enough I didn't question the way she acted. It just wasn't worth kicking up a fuss. It was released in 1939 just after Michael Balcon, head of MGM in Britain, formed a new film company using the Ealing studios. He named this company Ealing Studios, and it was here that classics such as *The Lavender Hill Mob* and *Kind Hearts and Coronets* would be made after the Second World War.

After a few months of variety and radio work, I returned to the studio to make my second film, *Let's Be Famous*, this time for the new Ealing Studios. *Let's Be Famous* was only the third film to be made by the company and was the very first 'Ealing comedy'. I'd enjoyed my first film so much that I was really looking forward to getting back into the swing of filming. Unfortunately making the second film was nowhere near as enjoyable.

Once again, I was the female lead but the plot was complicated. It centred around radio broadcasting and talent scouts. My character, Betty Barton, won a local crooning contest and was sent to London to sing at Broadcasting House. Betty's mother Polly Punch, an old variety performer, was also on the bill, along with a talent-less Irishman called Jimmy Houlihan who happened into the broadcast by mistake. Jimmy was played by Jimmy O'Dea who had been my love interest in *Penny Paradise*, and I was thrilled to work with him again.

The other lead part, that of a talent scout called Finch, was played by Sonnie Hale, brother of Binnie and just as obnoxious. I was wary about working with another Hale but luckily I didn't come into contact with him much during the filming. He'd been married to Evelyn Laye and the break-up of their marriage had caused a scandal. After our film he played romantic leads opposite Jessie Matthews and subsequently married her. The film was a knockabout comedy piece, which found us running around Broadcasting House trying to avoid each other and grabbing any chance we could to sing or crack gags on air. Quite bizarre!

Looking at the film again after all these years, the funniest thing is seeing all the BBC radio announcers talking into microphones dressed in dinner suits and bow-ties, as if the listeners could see them. But it was like that, very smart and proper, and so glamorous. When I first started in radio I always wore a lovely dress and smart men would introduce me in dashing dinner jackets. Older women would stand at microphones dripping in furs and diamonds. It made the evening special and very enjoyable.

I sang five songs in the film – 'I Ran Into Love', 'The Moon Remembered', 'I've Got a Hunch', 'Whistle When You Want Me' and 'The Gospel of Love' – and I can't remember the tune to any of them! Actually, I've probably blotted out my memories of the film.

It was wonderful being with Jimmy O'Dea again. He was a marvellous actor, who should have received more recognition than he did. Apart from Jimmy I wasn't impressed by the rest of the cast. Sonnie Hale was bumptious and full of his own importance – and then there was Lena Brown! She was cast as my mother and we loathed each another. I thought she was crude, and she didn't like the fact that I was billed higher than she was.

She had the most unsophisticated variety act in the world. All she did was stand on the stage, cracking filthy jokes and whistling. It wasn't subtle bird impressions or anything dainty, she'd shove her fingers in her mouth and let rip like a dockworker. I was eighteen at the time and she used to call me 'little Betty Driver'. It drove me up the wall and I was forever asking her not to, but she persisted. Some misguided person had thought her whistling was a novelty and that she might have the makings of a star. The poor director said he dreaded it every time she came on. She never delivered her lines as they were written, she'd stick gags in and start whistling as if she were on-stage. We had a scene, which eventually was cut out, that involved her getting on a train which I was already on. She had to walk along the platform, get on, talk to me and then the train moved off. Twenty-six takes it took. She just couldn't understand that it wasn't necessary to whistle during the scene or crack a gag whilst saying her lines. The director kept saying to her, 'Look, Lena, this is not a variety performance, this is a film and you are meant to be a real person. It isn't your act.' She just went on and on and on. Freda was an extra in that scene, sitting in the train carriage. It went on for so long that she read a whole book, from cover to cover, and fell asleep in the background.

As we were getting older, Mother loosened her hold on both Freda and me. Directors didn't want her hanging around the film sets so she'd wander off and make a nuisance of herself somewhere else, gossiping with the publicists or making a fuss over my costumes. Whilst they didn't welcome Mother, all the crew adored Freda and allowed her to sit and watch all my scenes. She was handy too, to sit in for me when I went to be dressed or made up. When the crew were sorting out the lighting on the sets Freda sat or stood in my place and ran my moves for them. She did this in both of my first films and it wasn't until the second was nearly finished that we realized the producers had been watching her 'performances'. She looked older than fifteen, was slim and classically beautiful, graceful and sophisticated. She had starlet written all over her. Secretly they filmed some of these lighting sessions and decided she had enough talent to merit a proper screen test as they had a film in mind for her.

The director's wife was selected to talk to Mother. She said she was taken with Freda and asked to take her to live in their apartment in Mayfair, saying that they would send her to RADA to be trained and groomed to go into pictures. Mother refused even to think about it and said, 'No, you're not turning my daughter into a tart.' Freda was heart-broken, and later on we discovered that the film they had wanted her for was *The Seventh Veil* with James Mason. The part was given to Ann Todd, who was much too old for the role and had to be made to look younger.

Mother was blinkered: she was interested in variety to the exclusion of all else. Films were like radio and records: they served to make me better known and therefore boosted my fees and billing in the theatre.

When Mother read the script for *Let's Be Famous*, she fell

upon a scene which said I had to have my photograph taken in the bath. She was concerned about this and made a nuisance of herself on the subject, challenging the director and the writer. As if they'd intended to film me naked! I had my own worries about the scene because Mother had always told me to keep myself covered, saying I had large limbs that shouldn't be seen. Because I'd heard this all my life, I believed it, and I refused to take my clothes off in front of everyone. For that scene I wore a strapless bathing suit, which wasn't seen because the bath water was covered with bubbles. All you could see of me was my head and shoulders! My mother behaved so stupidly during the filming of that scene and hung cloth around the bath so the crew wouldn't be able to see me in it. Silly woman!

In September 1939 we finished filming *Let's Be Famous* and war was declared on Germany. The studios closed down production and my contract with Ealing was cancelled. I was nineteen and, with Mother's plan of celluloid stardom not achieved, I was forced back to doing what I knew best – twice nightly in variety, touring the country with a couple of suitcases, Julie the Peke, Freda and my ever-present mother.

CHAPTER SIX

Variety – A Bill of Troupers

All through the years I spent in variety I was a timid little girl who should have been out playing with school-friends or reading at home. Instead I was living out of a suitcase and kicking my heels in short skirts in front of capacity audiences. I hated it, but looking back I realize I was fortunate to experience such a marvellous form of entertainment. I hit it when it was peaking and was just about to lose its battle against the cinema. I stayed with it until it died in the 1950s. I've shared billing with all the top acts and plenty of buffers too!

Variety invented itself from the dying embers of the old music-hall acts. Names like Vesta Tilly, Little Titch and Marie Lloyd had packed theatres with their rousing songs and daft jokes but as they fell away the entertainment business widened its arms to embrace the new acts of the 1930s. They came from all over the world to perform in England and this new art form was called variety, because that is what was offered on the bill: singers, comics, dancers, acrobats, animal acts, magicians, stunts, impersonators and musicians. This was the world I entered at twelve and stayed in for twenty years, until one by one the theatres emptied and turned into picture palaces or were knocked down to make way for office blocks.

The concept was simple and everyone knew exactly what they were doing. Each theatre was part of a group owned by a theatrical manager, who put on variety shows twice nightly. An artist's agent booked them to appear at various theatres or, if you were lucky, you might be engaged for a stint on a particular circuit of the theatres. Some were better than others. If you were good you were seldom out of work. I was unfortunate enough always to be in employment, and as I got older my billing changed, from 'Betty Driver, the Manchester Dynamo' to 'Manchester's Star Juvenile' and eventually 'Star of Radio and Film'.

Billings were important. They were the posters put up over the town to announce that week's show. The star had top billing, and the next star was at the bottom. In between came everyone else. There used to be about seven artists on a bill. The first turn to perform was often a couple of dancers, then a warm-up comic (Bill Waddington, the *Street*'s Percy Sugden, was often employed as a second comic), then more acts until the act before the interval, which would be whoever was bottom of the bill (or the co-star), then more acts after the interval, including the warm-up comedian again, and the top performer finished the show.

Before the end of the 1930s my name was at the top of the bill sheets. As well as your name you were always tagged with a strapline. Gracie Fields was often 'Lancashire's Lassie', Max Miller was 'the Cheeky Chappie', Tessie O'Shea was 'Two Ton Tessie', Max Bygraves 'Silly but Happy', and

Laurel and Hardy, who toured the UK in the 1950s, were 'Hollywood's Greatest Comedy Couple'. In August 1938, at the Manchester Hippodrome I was billed as 'Manchester's Star Juvenile – a Cute and Clever Kiddie in an Irresistibly Attractive Act.' A cute kiddie and I was eighteen! On the same bill the management proudly presented Teddy Brown, the Great Xylophonist, Silvestri, the World's Greatest Juggler, Three Crichton Boys and Beryl Evetts – 'Superb Soloists and Versatile Entertainers in Piano, Banjo and Saxophone, She Has 'Hap-hap-happy Feet' and George Betton, the Modern Comedian.

However they were billed, each artist travelled to a new theatre each week and went through the same routine of getting digs and acquainting themselves with the theatre. Each Monday afternoon found us gathered around the orchestra pit, having the band call, where you distributed your music to the band and had a quick run-through so they knew how you were going to sing or dance. Mother, and in later years, Freda, would take charge of these meetings, instructing the band on inclinations and telling the stage manager which lights would be needed to bring out the best in my skin tone and my dresses. I think I was pretty simple to deal with as I had no props or furniture. As a child I would sing in front of a curtain then later, when the act became more sophisticated, I had a grand piano on-stage with me and sang into a microphone on a stand.

It was lonely being a child in variety. When I wasn't sitting in my dressing room, watching the hours drag past, I would sneak down to the wings and watch the other acts, study their timing and the way they played the audience. That's how I learnt my trade. And there were so many to watch.

I adored comics. I even worked with one as his feed. It was the most enjoyable thing I ever did in variety and that was because I was working with the finest comic in the business, Robb Wilton. He was a grand old Liverpudlian gentleman with a fantastic wit. He used to travel everywhere with his wife, Florence, who used to appear in his acts. This one time she was ill, and Robb phoned my agent to see if I was free. I was delighted to be asked as I was his biggest fan. I joined the show and did a singing spot and a sketch with him set in a courtroom. He was the judge and I was the poor wretch in the dock. It was hilarious and we got more laughs than usual because his wife played it all with a straight face, but I kept cracking up and couldn't cope. He was incredibly funny and I was so upset when his wife was well enough to return to the act. He was the best.

Another old pro was Frank Randle and, although I never worked with him, I covered for him once. I was playing the Winter Gardens in Blackpool and the manager asked me to do my act at the North Pier as Frank, the star of that show, couldn't go on. I agreed and afterwards asked after Frank, concerned that he might be ill. The manager handed me a telescope and told me to look out to sea. I saw a little boat, with Frank sitting in it. Apparently he did this every time there was a full moon; it affected him like that. He just sat out there waiting for the full moon to finish. As a thank-you Frank bought me a drink in the bar. He ordered himself a Guinness and I was horrified when he took out his false teeth and placed them on the bar top. I said, 'Is that meant to be a gag?' but he said, 'No, it's for real, I can't drink anything unless I take all my choppers out.' He was a great northern comic, whose fame never really spread south of

Watford and who eventually ruined his reputation with heavy drinking.

One of the funniest acts I ever saw was Claude Williams. He was a pro's act: worshipped by those backstage more than those in the audience. He was forever getting the bird from the audience. He used to wear a velvet smoking jacket and did a conjuring act where everything went wrong, very like what Tommy Cooper did. Claude was talented, but was about thirty years before his time and the audiences didn't understand him. All the pros would stand at the side of the stage and watch, loving every minute. He'd have an easel with a blackboard and after every trick that went wrong he'd write on this board – 'Claude' – then 'The Great Claude' – then 'The Wonderful Claude'. We'd be in fits of laughter but the audience wouldn't raise a titter. A marvellous comic. If he was around now he'd make a fortune.

Nellie Wallace was a wonderful comedienne who always had me in hysterics. She was a Glaswegian who started her career as a clog dancer and did a wonderful comedy act. She always wore a funny little hat and a fur round her neck, which she referred to as 'my little bit of vermin'. She was a big star and earned a lot of money. I met her on a radio broadcast once, when she'd come out of retirement in her sixties. I'll never forget drooling over her diamonds. I gushed over them, saying I thought she was wonderful and begged her to show me her rings. She said, 'That's all I've got left.' Her husband had taken everything – the bank account, her furs, her home, everything. 'Thank God I never took my jewels off,' she added. That's why she'd had to start working again. She let me wear her rings during the broadcast. I really fancied myself with those diamonds on my fingers. Nobody knew how old Nellie really was as she was determined to keep her age a secret. In the 1948 Royal Variety Performance at the London Palladium she pirouetted energetically across the front of the stage. Later she collapsed backstage and died a few days later. It was only then it was discovered she was seventy-eight.

Issy Bonn was a fantastic Jewish comic and singer. His wife left him whilst we were working together at the Wood Green Empire, sharing the top of the bill. He was heartbroken and had to stop working. A few years later I went to see him in *Aladdin*. He played Abanaza, and it was a great show. He looked wonderful. However, in the middle of the cave scene, surrounded by heaps of jewels, he began to sing 'My Yiddisher Momma' – in *Aladdin*! But the audience was full of Jews, who loved it. It brought the house down.

Another great Jewish comic was Dave Morris. He was a lovely chap, very down-to-earth and ordinary, whose wife travelled with him. He didn't believe in banks so they carried all his money around in a great big Gladstone bag. One day his wife came to the theatre in a mink coat that was an inch from the floor. It consumed her and I told her she'd be better off having about two foot taken off it. It dragged along the pavement as she walked. She said, 'Bugger that, I've paid for it. It's stopping how it is.' Dave shrugged and said to me, 'I agree with you. Don't you think it's a little bit Jewish?' He was such a funny comedian.

One of my favourite modern comedians was Max Wall. I worked with him quite a few times. I remember seeing him at the Palladium. He was a brilliant dancer. He had a little set of steps only about a foot high and he'd do the smartest dance up and down them on the toes of his shoes. A wonderful tap routine, so dainty and agile. After dancing he got a little three-legged milking stool and sat with it right at the front of the stage with both his feet resting on the footlights and he'd play his guitar and sing. He was a star. The night I was in the audience everyone was laughing because his flies were undone and part of his shirt was sticking out. I felt so embarrassed for him, and he had no idea why the audience were laughing so much.

One sort of act I've always appreciated is a good drag performer. I've worked with many but will never forget seeing my first glamorous all-drag show. It was called *Soldiers in Skirts* and Mother took me to see it at a theatre in Stockport. It was a good show, full of dance and good routines, but one boy stood out from the rest. He was beautiful and very talented. After the show I went backstage and met all the lads, who were being rather bitchy towards the man I'd admired. I insisted on seeing him and knocked on his dressing-room door. And there he was, Daniel Carroll. I said, 'My dear, I think you're so beautiful, but I want to give you some advice. You make all this lot look like amateurs, and you stand out like a beautiful star. All you need to do is take all that tat off, that cheap dress and that awful wig. Spend a lot of money on a natural wig and get the finest couturier to make you a gown and matching shoes. Look after your nails, and think quality and find a good foundation.' So he did and within a year he was the toast of the drag world and changed his name to Danny La Rue. I was very touched when he wrote in his autobiography, 'It is through Betty Driver that I became what I am.' He really was the prettiest creature I'd ever seen in my life, lovely Dan.

I'm a huge fan of his. I couldn't tell you how many nights we've sat up together chatting.

Another boy, in that same show, was Terry Gardener, who befriended Danny. For many years I sold him my stage clothes and jewellery that I didn't want to keep.

There was another wonderful act, which had two fellas dressed as women, called Bartlett and Ross. Terry Bartlett was the comedy one, about as fat as a twig and always dressed in grotesque outfits. Colin Ross was Polish and very elegant. He would dress as a ballerina and danced in tutus, on pointe. You couldn't tell he wasn't a woman. I worked with them often and admired Colin's outfits. One day Terry offered to make me a dress. I bought some pretty material and he took all my measurements, both of us standing there in bras, knickers and feather mules. And I had no idea they were fellas, didn't have a bloody clue. I was so naïve! But I loved that dress. One week – after I'd discovered they were fellas – we were in Morecambe and they suggested we went to the open-air swimming pool as it was lovely weather. In those days I was slender, and Freda and I had lovely suits on. Colin wore tiny little shorts and looked gorgeous. But Terry, for some reason, wore a pair of knitted swimming trunks. He dived into the pool, then refused to come out: his trunks had filled with water and he couldn't keep them up. They were right down by his ankles and he was dragging them along, like a trawler's net. We hauled him on to a raft in the middle of the pool and the three of us sat round him whilst he wrung them out and put them back on.

That same week in Morecambe I was asked to judge a beauty contest. I can't bear those things but in those days, if asked I was always keen to help out. I was picked up in a huge Rolls-Royce and was driving along the front. Suddenly we stopped, and the driver said we had to pick up the Mayor and Mayoress. They owned a boarding house and there they were, with their chains and pinnies on, serving cod and chips to holiday-makers. When they got into the car the smell of chip fat made me feel sick. Then I had to sit on a podium between them whiffing of vinegar trying to look sophisticated.

A great drag act in reverse was that of the Houston sisters, Renee and Billie. Billie would dress as a boy and they did a sensational comedy singing act. Unfortunately Billie had to leave the act through illness but Renee carried on alone. She was one of the most generous people I've ever met. Once we had a big broadcast to do at the London Casino and when I arrived with my music there was a great commotion as Renee had appendicitis and they didn't think she'd be able to go on. Renee was determined to carry on. She was in awful pain but she sent her boyfriend to buy six hot water bottles and had them pinned inside her fur coat. She did her act wearing the coat and the bottles, which helped lessen the pain. After the show she collapsed and was rushed to hospital for an operation. But that's the sort of thing a true trouper did.

There weren't many ventriloquists on the circuits but the best was a young man called Arthur Worsley. I fell madly in love with him. He was a handsome boy from Manchester, tall and slim, and wore a dinner suit for his act. We went out together for a while and I would have liked to marry him but our mothers were like knives at each other all the time. They were two of a kind, both desperate to hang on to their

meal tickets and terrified we'd fall in love, marry, and they'd
lose control of us. They made our lives a misery. We tried to
meet in secret, with him travelling across the country to be
with me for snatched moments but it was no good: our
mothers were too alert. If we went for lunch our mothers
came, if we walked in the park they walked with us. He eventually married a woman called Audrey and had a child, but
his mother made their lives a nightmare. He'd never speak,
the dummy said it all, and try as you might you could never
see his lips move, not a muscle. He was the finest vent in the
world.

The most fun I had in variety was in the summer of 1938
when I was booked for the season at Blackpool. The show
was called *All the Best*, and I was glad to be settled at one
theatre for a few months. It was a big show with a wonderful
cast – Stanley Holloway, Elisabeth Welch, George Lacy, all
top liners. Of course, I knew Stanley from the Aza family
parties where he would perform his famous Edgar Marriott
monologue 'The Lion and Albert'. Although everybody
thinks of him as having an accent – particularly after his
performance as Eliza Dolittle's father in *My Fair Lady* – off-
stage he had hardly a trace.

There was also an elderly comedian called Billy Bennett,
who was sensational. He had an act in which he would
parody well-known songs. When the show opened he wasn't
very well. We worked on a big rostrum that went over the
orchestra, and all the artists had to walk out on to it. He was
nervous about going on because he couldn't see very well,
so when it was his turn I led him up to the microphone then
walked off again and went back for him when he'd finished.
He brought the house down, an absolute riot. When we

took our curtain call at the end, the only way I could get him on to the stage was to put my arm around him and lead him out. He so desperately didn't want anyone to know he was ill. That was the last night he ever worked. He'd taken a house for the summer in St Anne's with his girlfriend and had to go to bed, too ill to work. A few weeks later his body was found outside the house: he'd been out in the middle of the night, got out of his car and fallen face first into a puddle and died. He was a womanizer and all the profession said, 'That's where he should be, in the gutter,' but I took a different view and his death saddened me. He had been billed as 'Almost a Gentleman' and did wonderful comic monologues. He wore a Victorian tail suit with a white shirt bib, a blue garter sash across his front and hobnailed boots. His hair was parted and plastered down with grease. I've never heard an audience roar so much in my life. He was a master of what he did, wonderful.

During my time in Blackpool, we bade farewell to a member of the Driver troupe. Whilst I was making my first film we had bought a tortoise for threepence from a pet shop. We called him George and he stayed with us for about four years. He came everywhere with us – Freda carried him around in an old hatbox with straw inside it. We'd be driving along with George on the back seat and he'd push the lid off his box and peer out then climb on to Freda's lap to look out of the window to see where he was going. We'd get to digs and the first thing we'd ask was, 'Do you have a garden or yard where we can keep our tortoise?' These landladies must have thought we were daft.

During the season in Blackpool we rented a house and

every Sunday we'd invite all the chorus boys and girls round for tea and cakes and we'd sit out on the lawn and feed George: he used to beg for crumbs by pawing our legs with his front feet. We'd feed him strawberries and he'd answer to his name. We left him at our digs that summer because he went into hibernation and we couldn't find him. I was distraught and so was Freda, until the landlady said she'd look after him when he appeared and that we could collect him the next time we stayed, but we never went back to that place. I've often wondered what became of him. Tortoises can live for decades and perhaps he's still there – but I can't remember now where that house was.

During the run we all had to understudy each other. My understudy was a chorus girl who couldn't sing, and I had to understudy Elisabeth Welch, a famous black singer. One big scene was set in a gypsy camp: Stanley Holloway was the Gypsy king and there were colourful gypsy caravans on the stage. The scene involved the stealing of a child from a noble lady. The child's nanny was Elisabeth Welch, who came on dressed as an old-fashioned maid and sang a big number. One day she wasn't well so at a moment's notice, I had to take her role but there wasn't time to change. I did the song dressed in an exquisite full-length evening-gown. I enjoyed the scene and afterwards Stanley Holloway said, 'I wish you were doing that number every night,' and I said, 'I reckon I'll only be doing it the once.' I was right: Elisabeth Welch heard how well I'd been received and made damn sure she had recovered enough to go on the next night.

To modern audiences it is almost impossible to describe the lavish scale of these summer shows. The finale to *All the*

Best was a spectacular confection of thirties art-deco glamour, fans, feathers and showgirls. There must have been over forty people on the stage.

Whilst in the show I made friends with a troupe of exquisite French dancers, called the Demurrer Ballet. They had gorgeous eyelashes and showed me how to make them. They'd put two pins into the edge of the dressing-table, a few inches apart, pull out a hair, tie it to one of the pins then wrap it around both pins. Then they took another hair and crocheted it to the first hair with a tiny buttonhook, made a loop and pushed it under the other hair. Then they trimmed it into shape and rolled it on a pencil. Then it was ready to stick on with latex. I used my own hair first of all, then got a mane of Chinese hair to use. Oh, yes, nothing but the finest hair for Betty Driver's eyelashes!

Even though I was eighteen Mother's hold over me was still strong. She dictated everything I did, even what I wore. She was happy for me to wear short skirts and skimpy outfits on stage but when it came to life off-stage she laid down strict rules. I wasn't allowed low necks and if I was sitting in a room with anyone and my dress rose over my knee she'd bark, 'Cover yourself over. You're disgusting.'

Whilst in Blackpool Freda and I sneaked off to St Anne's in search of new shoes. Now, in Mother's mind anything above a court shoe made you a tart. We found these lovely high-heeled light blue sandals and bought a pair each. When we got home Mother went mad, told us both we looked like prostitutes. I immediately took mine off and never wore them again but Freda had more spirit. In an act of defiance she continued to wear those sandals until they fell apart and every time she put them on Mother said she looked like a tart. I marvelled at Freda's defiance and took courage from it. Mother began to realize she couldn't browbeat Freda as she did me and that was the turning point in my life . . . when Freda stepped out of the shadows to pull me free from Mother's iron grasp.

CHAPTER SEVEN

Loosening Mother's Hold

The outbreak of the Second World War in September 1939 stunned me. There I was, finally free from variety, starring in films, treated as a star, and suddenly all the studios were closed to become storage depots for the government. All contracts were immediately terminated. I tried to look on the bright side: I'd found filming more fun than variety but the slow process of setting lights, rehearsing then acting to fill just a few seconds' worth of film each day was too much. I'd always been an active girl and hanging around film sets with Freda could be dull. Also, Mother had started to upset rather a lot of people at Ealing and, although people didn't criticize her in front of us, I was uncomfortable with the way she behaved – as if she could direct my films better than anyone else.

So, it was back to the old routine of life in variety. I was nineteen, Freda sixteen and the idea of traipsing around with Mother filled us both with dread. At least whilst working at Ealing our domestic arrangements had borne some sense of normal life: we'd lived in the same house for more than a week and allowed ourselves the luxury of getting to know a community. Now we were back on the road again and in desperation I told Freda that I didn't think I could cope with it any more. I'd worked solidly, with only Sundays off, for over six years, and there was no sign of Mother giving me a holiday or easing the schedule. She was happy: *Penny Paradise* had been released and I was in demand in the top variety theatres. Now that I could be billed as 'film star', she could demand a higher fee for my act and the Azas had no trouble in filling my date book for the foreseeable future.

Since Freda had re-entered my daily life, I'd dared to hope that Mother would return to life in Manchester and allow us girls to travel together, with Freda looking after me. At night, tucked up in our shared bed in a rented room close to whichever theatre I was playing, Freda and I would plan our future. I'd tell her how much I hated the music Mother made me sing, the same silly routine I'd been stuck with since I was thirteen. Freda understood, and was in tune with the sort of bright, modern numbers I longed to sing. She would hold me tight and, as I cried into the pillow, she'd swear that one day we'd get rid of the songs – and Mother.

Nineteen thirty-nine saw me making my début in a fashionable new medium called television. The BBC were making occasional programmes, which were shown only in London, and I was asked to be a guest on a show. At the time I was appearing at the Dudley Hippodrome, topping the bill with a male singer called David Whitfield. He was a handsome man who made famous the beautiful ballad 'I Believe'. I travelled down to London for a few days with

Freda and Mother because the television show was to be rehearsed and broadcast live from the London Coliseum. As you can imagine, Mother was terribly excited because here was another means of spreading my name to the masses. I'd have thought that, what with variety, films, records and radio, the public were sick of my name by then. I'd been making records continuously; just darting into studios, cutting them and never hearing them. I never liked the sound of my own voice, and years later, in an act of rage against what Mother had forced me to do, I smashed all the records Freda had so lovingly collected.

As soon as we arrived at our digs in London, Mother opened her case and out tumbled all the old band parts I loathed, the ones that were silly and girlish, and stuck in my throat to sing. The worst one was a comedy song/monologue that she'd had written for me. It was awful. She happily sorted the band parts into neat piles, chatting away about how wonderful it would be for me to be on television, and all the time I was staring at her, my eyes watering at the thought of singing those hideous songs. Freda didn't say anything, she just sat there watching me and Mother. Then she asked Mother, 'Is that the lot? All of them?' Mother said it was. Quick as a flash, Freda leapt forward, grabbed all the music in her arms and threw the lot on the fire. I just stood there, my mouth open in amazement as I watched the flames licking around the sheets of paper. Mother screeched and thrust her hands into the fire to rescue the music but she was too late. My whole act went up in flames in front of our eyes. I was terrified as Mother vented her anger on Freda. She flew at her, lashing out at her with her hands and fingernails. She was screaming like a banshee and all hell broke loose. It was awful. I just shrank into the background. In her anger Freda actually hit back at Mother, and afterwards when Mother told people in the theatre that Freda had struck her they all cheered.

It took a long time to calm Mother down and for Freda to explain the songs were all wrong for me. Mother was beside herself with rage. How dare Freda criticize the music that had been feeding and clothing us! How dare she criticize Mother's choice!

But Freda hadn't finished. Having seen off the music she turned her attention to my clothes. Mother always dressed me in these little taffeta girly frocks with nipped waists, high straps and collars, and Freda stood up and said, 'You can't dress her in those. This is the West End stage, not a charity show. She's got to have something smart and modern.' Mother couldn't handle this: no one had stood up to her before, not her parents, Dad or me, and here was sixteen-year-old Freda fighting back with an anger that matched her own. I couldn't believe it: it was more than I could ever have hoped for. Freda just snapped. She thought enough was enough and that if she didn't stand up for me I'd be worked into the grave. I fully expected Mother to kill her, I really did, and was amazed when she simply threw her hands in the air and shouted, 'On your back be it. I'm not having anything to do with it. You think the dresses are no good, you get new ones!' I couldn't believe she'd backed down so quickly. Perhaps she realized Freda was prepared to fight her every inch of the way until she gave in.

The next morning Freda and I walked all over London looking in shop windows. It was as if a weight had been lifted from my shoulders and as I looked at all the beautiful dresses in these very grand stores I couldn't believe we were actually going to buy one for me. In Grosvenor Square we came across a beautiful shop called Anthony Gills. In the window was a beautiful dinner gown, an unpleated full-length skirt of two shades of delicate grey and a little cherry-red waisted top, short sleeves. I fell in love with it straight away. I tried it on and knew I looked sensational, but it was a dinner dress and singers didn't wear dinner dresses: we wore evening gowns. Freda insisted we bought it. When mother saw it she was furious, screaming, 'No one wears a dinner dress on the stage!' Freda took no notice. We went back into London and picked new songs for me, sophisticated numbers to match my new gown. She chose them and I trusted her. Mother thought the whole idea of me attempting to be sophisticated and glamorous was laughable and refused to have anything to do with the television appearance, so Freda took me to the theatre without her. I was a bag of nerves as I was rehearsing my new songs and waiting to go on. Freda sat in the transmission van with the technicians and saw me appearing on their black and white monitors, looking knockout in my new dress and gliding through my numbers.

I stood on the stage, as normal, lit by a spotlight, and the huge television camera stood by the orchestra pit. There was just the one camera and when I had a close-up the operator quickly changed the lens. It was just an ordinary, straightforward performance for me, I had no need to be nervous at all. The only difference was that the microphone that stood in front of me was enormous and I had to keep darting around it to be seen. During the rehearsal I'd taught myself how I needed to stand, depending on how low my notes were going to be. The only way to control the level of noise recorded was for me to sway backwards and forwards depending on how I was singing.

It was wonderful and Mother couldn't say anything to condemn me, the dress or the songs because the next day *The Times* reviewed the show, saying, 'Beautifully gowned Betty Driver sets a new trend in clothes on the stage, in a glorious dinner dress.' After that *everyone* wore dinner dresses.

Overnight my act had changed. Gone were the immature songs, imitations of Gracie Fields and frilly dresses. Now I was a ballad singer, and the songs Freda chose for me to sing each week were brand new. Suddenly music publishers were interested in me. Denmark Street in London was where all the major publishers had their offices – Chappells, Sterling, Francis Day & Hunter, Edwin Morris, Bradbury Wood. Now I was in demand as a singer of the sort of songs they were trying to sell they would telephone and invite me to visit their offices to look over the new numbers they had bought. They all kept grand pianos and a pianist would play a song for me. Freda and I would know immediately whether it was right for me or not. I'd tell the pianist to lower or raise the key and would say, 'I'm doing a broadcast on such a day and I want this number. There's twenty-six in the band and I want to start with the verse, then do the chorus and then go back half a chorus and finish with a crescendo at the end.' Then they would get the music written up into band parts, especially for me, for free. Also, they had my photograph and would print the music with my face on the cover and sell it all over the country. People would see me on the stage, or listen to my broadcasts then go out and spend a shilling on the music. From the moment Freda took over from Mother to the last recording I made in the late 1950s hundreds of these music sheets were printed. Now people send them to me occasionally and I can't remember the songs at all. I look at my face on the cover and read the lyrics and follow the score but have no recollection of them.

There was a practice in the music publishing industry called song-plugging, which I refused to get involved in. A representative from a firm would call at my dressing room and say, 'We've got a number which is just you,' and offer me twenty-five pounds to take it and use it. The firm would be desperate to have the number associated with a well-known singer but I never accepted the money or the songs. Some people made a fortune out of this, before it was made illegal.

One song became particularly associated with me and turned into something of a signature tune. It was called 'The Sailor With The Navy Blue Eyes'. I grew to hate it but the audiences loved it.

Having established my new 'look' I was keen to buy more dresses, but they were so expensive. Once again, Freda came to the rescue. She decided it couldn't be that difficult to make them and started to travel with a little Singer sewing machine. We'd flick through *Vogue* and *Harper's Bazaar* and I'd point out the dresses I liked. Freda would adapt patterns and make them up for me. She had had no training and taught herself how to do it. She cut them out on the dressing-room floor then pinned them together with me inside and sewed them on to me so they were a perfect shape.

The first one she made was a favourite of mine. Dark

maroon, it had an extra flounce on the front and she beaded the sleeves. It looked gorgeous and I was so eager to wear it that I insisted on keeping it on after a fitting to go on stage even though it was held together at the back with huge nappy-pins. She said, 'For God's sake, back off, don't turn round.' She used to dye my shoes the same colours as the dresses. The press reporters were always commenting on my gowns and trying to find out where I bought them. I'd keep quiet and just smile at Freda.

CHAPTER EIGHT

I Fall In Love

By 1940 Mother was still part of my travelling act, though she had backed off a bit, and I was still treading the boards twice nightly in touring variety and grumbling to Freda about how much I hated it. By now I'd done variety, revue, straight plays, radio, records, films and television. I thought I'd covered everything but Mother still had an ace up her sleeve: pantomime!

I have never liked pantomime. In proper pantomime the principal boy and girl are both played by women and I always found it detestable to see them kissing on-stage. I'd always refused to consider appearing in pantomime because Mother had always told me to keep my legs covered because they were too fat. One day my agent, Lillian, called me into her office on Charing Cross Road, in London, and made me try on different pairs of tights so she could see these terrible legs for herself. I put on the tights and she said my legs were perfect, but it made no difference: I'd listened to my mother's criticism so much I believed every word of it. Lillian had had an offer for me to appear in *Robin Hood* at the Theatre Royal, Hanley but I wouldn't consider the idea, saying there was no way I was playing principal boy. She stopped me in my tracks and asked if I'd consider playing principal girl. Ten minutes later she'd talked me into it. As I returned home on the train I told myself I was a complete and utter fool.

The pantomime ran for six weeks over Christmas and I was to play Maid Marian, opposite Dorothy Penny as Robin Hood. Dorothy was a fabulous artist, a tall, beautiful girl. It soon became obvious in rehearsals that both of us had been miscast. I was never dainty or feminine and next to me her Robin Hood looked a right pansy! Still, we went on and I have to say I enjoyed the experience. Hanley was a wonderful place to play: the people were kind and gentle and they wrapped round me. It was a pleasure playing to them. However, towards the end of the run I started to suffer from a nervous complaint. Put plainly, I developed severe stage fright. A week before the run finished I was on-stage and suddenly felt very strange. As I was singing I thought the audience were staring and pointing at me. It terrified me so much I had a blackout and fainted. The stage manager dropped the curtain and I was dragged into the wings where Mother threw a cup of water in my face and told me not to be silly. She forced me to go on again but as soon as it came to another song I blacked out again. The third time it happened a doctor in the audience leapt up. Mother told him I was only faking and tried to manhandle him away, but he stood his ground and insisted I went home, saying I was seriously ill. I was exhausted from working without a break for years, but Mother refused to let me rest and insisted I went back to work.

The management at Hanley were more sympathetic than

With Freda, my sister and best friend.

My first appearance in front of a camera, aged two-and-a-half.

The wedding of my parents, Frederick and Nellie, in 1919.

My beloved grandparents, George and Polly Driver, whose country garden was an oasis for me as a child.

A family gathering at Bradgate Park, Leicester. In the foreground (l-r) are father, me and mother; at the back (l-r) are two aunts, Freda and cousin Joyce.

Mother used her position on the Co-op committee to have me entertain retired policemen all over Manchester.

Mimicking Gracie Fields in front of the dirty old men at The Prince of Wales (above).

At fourteen, London's youngest leading lady, in *Mr Tower of London* (right).

Signed up as a film star at the tender age of seventeen – a career cut short by the outbreak of war (opposite).

A publicity still for *Sis Hopkins* – shortly before I stormed off to the railway station with my packed bag.

Glitz and glamour at a preview for one of my films. Posing for the Press before Mother grabbed the bouquet.

Let's Be Famous,
1939, with (l-r)
Jimmy O'Dea,
Sonnie Hall and
Basil Radford.

My face appeared
on hundreds of
song sheets and I
can't remember
any of them!

SAM'S SONG
(THE HAPPY TUNE)

Words by JACK ELLIOTT

Music by LEW QUADLING

Featured & Broadcast by
BETTY DRIVER

THE STERLING MUSIC PUBLISHING CO. LTD
50 NEW BOND ST, LONDON, W.1.

Where I felt most comfortable – standing behind a microphone.

Relaxing with dear Henry Hall, the kindest man in the world.

Mother, though, and they allowed me to finish the run early. I had nothing booked until after the pantomime was due to finish so I was looking forward to a week's rest. Mother, however, wasn't happy and persuaded the Azas to book me to appear in *The Billy Cotton Club*, a radio show broadcast from Bristol. Soon after confirming the booking the BBC telegraphed to ask if I could change my plans and deputize for a singer who was working with Henry Hall's orchestra. Henry was the BBC's resident band leader and had a huge following with listeners. Each week he broadcast a big concert and this week it was coming from Cheltenhem.

I wasn't happy with the idea of performing when I felt so low, especially with an orchestra I didn't know. Still, Mother bundled me into the car and off we drove. I arrived and introduced myself to Henry, a tall, earnest-looking chap with receding hair and glasses. He looked like the typical university professor, and I was rather scared of him. He saw I was clutching my music to my chest and he asked to see it. I mumbled that it was only pit-band orchestrations, but he smiled, took the sheets of paper from me and said it was all right.

I looked at his smiling face and blurted out how much I adored him and his band, and apologized once again for the band parts, saying I only did variety. He told me not to worry and handed them out to the band, who all made fun of the music. Henry let them have a little snigger then told them to improvise. I went to get changed and stood in the wings waiting to be introduced. It was a packed theatre and the microphone on the stage was linked directly to the BBC transmission suite, which would beam my voice all over the country.

I'd done concerts like this before but never with a full orchestra behind me and my legs turned to jelly. Somehow I walked on to the stage and stood waiting for the introduction to my first number. The orchestra started and I couldn't believe what I was hearing: my music sounded magnificent! Straight away my nerves left me and I launched into song and had a ball! Afterwards Henry was as pleased as I was and said he was sorry I couldn't stay on with him but his singer, who was ill, would have recovered in time for the next broadcast. I was just thrilled to have had the chance to sing with his fabulous orchestra.

For the first six weeks of 1941 my time was split between touring in the revue *Twice In A Blue Moon* and spending my Thursday evenings appearing in a variety radio show for the BBC called *Radio Boost*. I'd sing two songs and be paid fifteen guineas plus a third-class return fare from London and fifteen shillings subsistence allowance for overnight accommodation.

It was during my six-month run in *Twice In A Blue Moon* that Freda and I finally parted company with Mother. She came with us as I toured the country – although petrol was rationed, I was allowed supplementary coupons because we travelled to shows during the night and I was meant to be keeping up public morale. Freda and I had developed into a strong unit and half the time didn't notice Mother. She had cardiac asthma and could hardly walk, but she refused to leave us alone and return to Dad in Manchester.

During the war I performed in towns where I wouldn't usually go: all the city theatres were closed and we'd go to wherever the army camps were stationed close by. One week we were in Dewsbury, playing to soldiers and staying in some digs with Mother, who couldn't go upstairs. She'd never sleep on her own and always made me sleep with her. At two in the morning she woke me up, saying she needed the toilet. She wouldn't go upstairs to the toilet and insisted we got the car out and drove round Dewsbury looking for a ground-floor public lavatory that was open. It took us an hour and a half, and I was exhausted afterwards. When we got up the next morning Freda insisted that she was just too much to deal with and kept on and on at her to go home. Freda was frustrated because she saw her job as taking care of me but she couldn't do that properly because Mother's illness took up so much of her time. Now Freda refused to listen to Mother's protests and sent for Dad. He took her home and she was immediately admitted to hospital, where she stayed for six weeks. Before she agreed to leave us, she produced a Bible and made us both put our hands on it and swear we wouldn't go out with men. Freda had her fingers crossed and I crossed my legs! After that, we had to phone her every night to tell her we were all right. And finally I started to have fun, all thanks to Freda. It was then that I became dependent on her, and I've stayed so ever since.

It was during the tour of this revue that I first experienced the horrors of war. Up to that point the introduction of rationing in January 1940 had been our only hardship. Now we were journeying around the country and witnessing the devastation inflicted by the German bombers. When we arrived in Liverpool Freda and I were caught up in a raid for the first time. From then on, for the next few years, the bombs seemed to follow us wherever we went. It became the norm for stage managers everywhere to instruct us that if we were on stage and the siren went off the show had to carry on. However, if there was a serious threat overhead, the manager would interrupt to announce that everyone must leave the theatre. This happened that time in Liverpool. In the middle of my act the manager cleared the theatre and everyone ran down to the basement. There was no panic, no stampede: the audience were resigned to the bombs and we just followed their lead. Whilst in Liverpool we performed at a theatre in Bootle, as the main theatres in the city had been smashed to the ground.

Poor Bootle, it suffered badly from the bombs. I remember that whilst we were there we had digs in an old terraced house, sharing with a troupe of children who were in the show, and looked after by a matron. The sirens blared out all night long, and we'd sit in the landlady's basement shelter, singing to the children. There'd be me, Freda and another girl in the show, a Scottish lass called Tina, who was a stripper with the most sensational figure and had a speciality act with fans. The landlady had turned the cellar into a comfortable little room, with beds for her boarders. We didn't spend a single night in our rooms. We had to keep our gas masks with us but they were ugly things so Freda covered their boxes with material to match our outfits – a bit of leopardskin, some satin, diamanté. Each night we'd grab these boxes and put on our siren suits, which I'd had made especially for us. They were very warm navy outfits, trousers and tops all in one with a big zip. Of course, I'd insisted on having the hoods lined with pale blue satin. We were such a conceited pair.

When *Twice In A Blue Moon* came to an end I returned to variety, touring around. We opened in Coventry

Hippodrome in a show the day after the blitz there and I've never experienced anything so heartrending. The whole city was charred and ruined, and the people wandered around like zombies. Sharing the bill with us that week were the Andrews family – father Bob, mother Barbara and little Julie, who would come on in a pretty frock and sing. She spent the entire week with Freda and me, terrified of the bombs that continued to fall around us. But we were there to do a job, to entertain. Even if there were only three people in the audience you made yourself up, got dressed up and did your act. I'll never forget little Julie . . . a lovely girl. And twenty years later there she was singing her heart out in *The Sound of Music*, bless her.

I continued to make regular trips to Bristol to sing on a half-hour comedy radio show called *Ack Ack Beer Beer*. It was a topical knockabout show full of sketches and spirit-lifting songs. I sang, accompanied by the show's pianist, the talented Kay Cavendish. Because of the blitz on London all the entertainment shows were moved out of Broadcasting House and were made at any available studio, makeshift theatre or town hall. I did many recordings in Bristol throughout the war and it was whilst I was there that I met Jack Watson for the first time.

Jack was five years older than me. He'd been in variety for years, in a double act with his father called 'Nosmo King and Hubert'. When the war started Jack became a PT instructor in the Navy. He was very fit and went on to represent England in springboard championships. Although he was in the Navy, he was given blocks of six weeks off on the understanding that he would entertain in venues around the docks. He was a semi-regular in *Ack Ack Beer Beer* and as soon as I saw him I fell head over heels in love with him. We did one broadcast together then were booked on the same bill the following week in Plymouth. His act was made up of songs, dances and plenty of patter. Incidentally, a young Canadian band-leader called Hughie Greene was also on the bill, but romance blossomed for me with Jack over that week.

We started going out together. He drove a little Austin Seven and had a crafty way of getting round petrol rationing: he'd put in a teaspoonful of petrol and fill the rest of the tank with paraffin. It was illegal and the car stank but it gave us opportunities to escape from the city. He used to drive me out to the Mendip Hills and we'd sit there watching the bombs falling on Bristol, playing jazz records on a wind-up gramophone on the back seat.

Somehow Jack arranged things so that both he and I were booked to play Bristol for a six-week run. Freda and I rented a room in an old terraced house in the city, half-way up a hill, and I threw myself into having a boyfriend, my first! The bombing was awful: we had raids that lasted thirteen hours each night, week after week. Most nights after the show, Jack would take Freda and me out for supper or a walk, but one night Freda decided she'd had enough of playing gooseberry and insisted we went to the pictures without her. We left her in the house, giving the landlady's daughter a singing lesson, and drove off into the city centre.

The bombing started so we returned earlier than planned. When we came back to the house we opened the front door and Jack fell straight through into the back garden: a stray bomber had flown over and dropped its full load on the terrace. Thankfully Freda had sensed something was going to happen and, seconds before the bombs hit she had flung herself and the child across the room towards the front of the house. The bombs split the house in half and when the rescuers came they found her standing by the front door clutching my band parts.

Of course, I didn't know what had happened and when I saw half the house missing I was certain Freda was dead. I became hysterical and started running down the hill, screaming. Jack tore after me, managed to calm me down, and the ARP men took me up the road to where Freda was. In those days she had long hair down to her waist and its colour had changed from black to white. I stared at her and said, 'Oh, my God, Jack, she's gone white with fright,' but it was only plaster dust. I was so relieved to find she was all right but both her legs were jet black from toe to hip with bruising.

Jack took charge of us, drove us out to Weston-Super-Mare and found us a place to stay. I phoned Mother and told her about the raid and Freda's legs, but she shrugged it off and said the bruising would heal and she shouldn't see a doctor. Ten years later we discovered that Freda's hip was dislocated. As it had been untreated she had to have two years of treatment.

The shows we made for the BBC were put together in what would seem today a very haphazard fashion. Most of the *Ack Ack Beer Beer* broadcasts were made from the same little church hall in a suburb of Bristol. Despite the constant bombing we always managed to broadcast the shows without stopping. Even when sirens were shrieking out and the planes were droning overhead we carried on, keeping a wary eye on the head technician. If he jumped up we knew the bombs were heading our way and that we would have to run.

Once we narrowly escaped with our lives. I'd just finished singing and the announcer was standing by the microphone in his penguin suit saying, 'You've been listening to so-and-so,' and the planes were flying overhead, the noise getting louder and louder. I ran off the stage and found Freda, who was holding our handbags, and together we darted out of the hall with the orchestra and Jack. The announcer carried on speaking but picked up speed and as soon as he'd said, 'Goodnight,' he legged it after us. Just as he reached the door a bomb hit the hall and demolished it.

We were never scared; it was simply part of the whole thing. It was our job to entertain, right up to the last minute, and we did so without question. Freda spent every broadcast sitting with the band parts, our coats and our handbags. Throughout the war she was known as 'our Freda with the handbags'. Every lady with whom I did a wartime broadcast left her handbag with Freda for safe keeping. It shows how trusted Freda was as a true pro never leaves her handbag anywhere. Even now I'm never without my handbag. I even take it to bed with me. A few months ago I had the shock of my life when locking up for the night I discovered Freda had left her handbag sitting on the hall table. I woke her up and said, 'You've left your handbag in the hall.' She was horrified!

The other thing about Freda at this period was that she seemed to radiate safety and a watchword grew up in the profession: if you were on the bill with Betty Driver, 'walk with Freda and you'll be safe'. We'd come out of our digs to walk to the theatre and there'd be groups of pros hanging around waiting for Freda. We went everywhere in gangs. It was amazing. She was like a lucky charm. She was never frightened of the bombs, and it might sound strange but there was an air of excitement about the war. We got used to the bombs, and the knowledge that any day might be your last bonded us all together.

As with the rest of the coastal cities, Bristol was pounded and eventually the bombing got to us to the extent that we decided to go to Manchester for a weekend, just for a good night's sleep. Needless to say we picked the worst weekend and poor Manchester suffered a horrific blitz. We travelled back to Bristol on the train during the Sunday night. When we arrived at Temple Meads Station at midnight it was on fire. The train drew in and was quickly evacuated. We refused to go down into the shelter and set off, on foot, to reach our digs. Freda and I walked through the city and watched the historic buildings blaze. We clung together and wept for it, stepping over fire hoses and debris. The firemen kept shouting at us to take cover but we lugged our suitcase along, rushing to get home. Every building was on fire and it took us three hours to walk to our lodgings.

At the time I had a lovely car, a Humber, and as we couldn't get petrol – even though we had a supplementary ration – it was garaged in a warehouse in the centre of the city. In the morning the landlord went into town and discovered our car safe and sound in one of the only buildings not to be bombed. It was amazing: all that bombing and it didn't have a scratch on it.

In May 1941 I turned twenty-one and for the first time took responsibility for my own money. Up to then my wages had been paid directly to my mother and she gave me pocket money. Originally five shillings a week, then ten and then, when I was about nineteen, a pound. Mother also paid Freda half a crown for being my companion. From that we had to buy our own makeup, stockings and other bits and pieces, whilst she swanked around in furs. During all that time my average weekly pay was fifty pounds a week, sometimes as much as a hundred and fifty. Freda insisted I took charge of my own finances so we went to Manchester and asked my parents to hand over my bank book and the accountancy books they'd been keeping for me.

We waited for the explosion but none came. Instead the books were handed over and I gave them to an accountant, who discovered I didn't have a penny to my name. My parents had carefully paid the income tax for me then spent all my money on drink, cars and clothes. I'd been working for all those years and had nothing to show for it. I was shocked and furious, and so was Freda. She'd been tied to me and unable to lead her own life as she had no money. Like me she had struggled to maintain relationships with boyfriends against Mother's wishes and failed. She had given her whole life over to looking after me. She was the strong-willed one and she fought for me, and I'd always thought I'd be able to pay her back, financially at least. But I had nothing to give her.

In the summer of 1941 I made my third and last film, *Facing the Music*. I signed a one-picture contract with Butcher's Film Services and was paid the handsome sum of a thousand pounds. As Mother had been handling my money before this I have no idea what I was paid for my other films. Filming took place at Elstree Studios and my co-star was an actor called Bunny Doyle. He was a famous dame and had more or less adopted the Yorkshire village of Giggleswick, where he said they were fond of playing tiddly-winks with manhole covers. In the film he played a man called Wilfred Hollibon, who was highly incompetent at his job. The Government decided to open a false munitions works to fool enemy spies and he was put in charge of it. I played his girlfriend and had little to do except sing a song entitled 'You Don't Have To Tell Me I Know'. Needless to say Wilfred ended up fooling the spies and was proclaimed a national hero. I don't remember anything else about the film, or making it. I don't think I enjoyed it much and have never seen it.

Whilst making *Facing the Music*, things finally came to a head with Jack. Our relationship had continued to develop and I was hoping he would propose, However, Mother, during a visit, put a stop to the romance once and for all. He came to see me at Elstree but Mother wouldn't allow the gate-keeper to let him in. She refused to let me out of the dressing room to see him but somehow Freda slipped out. He'd travelled miles to be with me and she wasn't going to let him be put off by Mother. To kill the afternoon Freda took him to the cinema then booked him into the Elstree country club where we were staying. He'd brought me a bootful of flowers, and after filming we went back to the club and there he was, with a beautiful spray of roses for me and his gorgeous smile.

Mother was furious: she thought Freda had got rid of him. You see, so long as I remained single I continued to be her meal ticket and she didn't want me to be involved with anyone. She created such a scene at the country club, shouted at him, then grabbed the roses out of his hand and threw them in his face. She made such a fuss that Jack and I had to acknowledge it was no good. At that time I was under Mother's thumb and didn't have the guts to stand up for myself or Jack. So we broke up. I would have married him if he'd asked but I didn't have the strength to fight a matriarch. She was a devil. I was heartbroken and wept for days.

Shortly after this Jack started work on a show called *Navy Mixture* in London. During the course of the show he met a BBC engineer called Betty Edwards, a lovely lady, and married her. He brought her to see me once after a show at the Bristol Hippodrome. Whilst I was writing this book Jack died, aged eighty-five. I was deeply saddened, but glad that he and Betty had had so many happy years together.

After *Facing the Music* my agent contacted me with the exciting news that Henry Hall had asked if I would join his band as his resident singer. *Would I?* It was like asking a little girl if she'd like to meet a fairy. I couldn't say 'yes' quickly enough. I started with him the next week and it was just as if I'd been transported from the slums to Buckingham Palace.

CHAPTER NINE

Happy Days With Henry Hall

Before every house boasted a television set, the wireless catered for the entertainment of the average family. *Dick Barton, The Ovaltinies, Band Wagon, ITMA, Tony Hancock,* the list of popular programmes was endless. The BBC dominated the airwaves and the personalities working for the Corporation were huge stars. One of the leading lights was Henry Hall, who conducted the BBC's resident dance band and had a huge following.

When I joined the band as lead vocalist it was a dream come true. It was glamorous. It was sophisticated. It was all I could have dreamt of and, to top it all, Mother had stepped out of my professional life and returned to Rusholme for good. Suddenly Freda and I entered a magical world, where I was a star performer and treated like royalty. All the music publishers wanted me to sing their songs, all the dressmakers implored me to wear their creations. It was a fabulous time for the little kid who'd been forced on-stage to mimic Gracie Fields!

Henry was forty-two when I first met him, a very English gentlemen who wore classically tailored suits and round, thin-rimmed spectacles. He'd started his musical career as a pianist, playing and leading the resident band at Manchester's Midland Hotel. At an early age he'd been made musical director for the company LMS Hotels and had controlled their thirty-two dance bands all over the country. In 1924 he began broadcasting on the then new wireless, and in 1932 became director of the BBC Dance Orchestra. Many people thought he was an odd person to pick for the job because the world was being flooded by jazz, swing and bop, but he refused to bow to the influx of this modern music and insisted on sticking to what he believed the listeners were most interested in. The music he chose was based on the experience he had gained throughout the country, of watching the public's reaction to melodies and tunes. He was proved right.

Henry was the first person to give a dance music broadcast from Broadcasting House when it was erected in 1932. Throughout the thirties, forties and fifties he played nearly three thousand hours on the air. In 1934 his band performed live on-stage for the first time, in a Royal Command Performance at the London Palladium. After this he moved the band into variety performances and took them on tour all over the world.

For the seven years I worked with Henry we stuck to a strict routine. We moved around the country playing at different venues each week, normally a theatre but sometimes a church hall or cinema. The first half of the show was standard variety – comics, singers, jugglers – then, during the interval, the band would come on to the stage and

Henry would conduct them throughout the whole of the second half, together with three vocalists. I'd come on right at the close and sing three numbers. Henry would start off with something nice and bright then a vocalist would join in, then another band number and so on until my spot, twice nightly. Every Thursday, between seven thirty and eight, the second half of the show would be broadcast live, from whichever theatre we were appearing at. These broadcasts were called *The Henry Hall Guest Night*: anyone who was available would be booked to perform between the band numbers, and I'd stand on the side of the stage and watch these brilliant performers until it was my turn to sing at the end of the broadcast. Comedians like Ted Ray, Arthur Askey and Max Miller would do their routines, and serious actors, such as Laurence Olivier, Rex Harrison, Noël Coward and John Gielgud, would deliver monologues or read poetry. Beautiful. The shows normally ended with Henry playing the piano and me singing with him.

Guest Night gave me the chance to work with huge stars who wouldn't normally have crossed my path in variety. Some were people I'd always admired, some were international stars and one was someone I thought I'd never see again. Henry came to me one day and asked if I'd mind sharing my dressing room with that week's guest. Binnie Hale. Her name could still intimidate me but because Henry had asked, and he was so good to me, I agreed.

It was over five years since our last meeting and her sun had definitely set. No longer was she the huge star, and when she arrived in my dressing room she looked sheepish. She put her bag down, cleared her throat and said quietly,

'Wasn't I a cow to you?' I looked at her and said, 'Yes.' She gestured round the dressing room and said, 'But you've got your own back now, haven't you?' I smiled and said, 'Too true.' The tables had turned. I was the star and she wasn't. That night we chatted away like old friends and I think I laid a ghost to rest.

Binnie only did the one *Guest Night* but others became regulars, like the old music-hall performer George Robey, who was generally thought of as the master comic of the early 1900s. All I can say is that I found him a most objectionable man. The first time we met him he started touching Freda up at the side of the stage so she hit him and called him a dirty old man. I didn't like him or his bawdy comedy. He billed himself as the 'Prime Minister of Mirth' and believed he was on a par with God. We'd be standing in the wings with the band, getting ready to go on, and he'd push us aside saying, 'Stand back, I'm a big star.'

Another popular act I wasn't fond of was performed by Elsie and Doris Waters. Like George Robey, they were regulars on *Guest Night* as Henry was a little bit old-fashioned and loved their act. They took on the personas of two Cockney women, Gert and Daisy, and would sit on stage together swapping banter in very long sketches. They were exceptionally good at it but I was into all things modern and couldn't see the sense of them. It wasn't slick enough for me. Off-stage they were very refined, spoke well and didn't mix with the rest of us – although they always gave Freda their handbags to watch over.

One of my favourite actresses appeared in one *Guest Night*: Evelyn Laye. I adored her. She was a huge star in musical comedy and made famous the song 'Lover Come

Back To Me'. When Henry asked if I'd share my dressing-room with her I went weak at the knees. She was one of the most beautiful women I'd ever seen, gorgeous fair hair and very delicate skin. In her act she always wore what was known as a Grecian gown, in pink, very smooth and draped around her so that it was nearly impossible to wear anything beneath it as it showed every line. I said to her, 'I don't know how you manage to wear those dresses and show no lines,' and she told me her secret. She wore long-legged latex knickers that ran from her waist to below her knees, which gave her this wonderful smooth outline. We got on famously together and after she did the broadcast she gave me a little present. I'm sorry to say I can't remember what it was!

Another of my favourites was the singer Anne Shelton. Like me, she was a dance-band vocalist, singing with Ambrose and his band for their broadcasts from London's Mayfair Hotel. Freda and I used to see quite a bit of her when we were in London. We understood her because she was dominated by her father in much the same way as I had been by Mother. During the war, Denmark Street was the place to see music publishers and try out different songs. Freda and I would meet Anne looking for music and we'd sneak off behind her father's back and have a coffee some-where. Her singing voice was much deeper than mine so luckily we never clashed over music. Anne used to sing slow numbers, similar to the ones favoured by Vera Lynn. My style was classed as 'popular' – ballads and comedy numbers. I can truly say that there was no competition or rivalry between any of us female vocalists and we all became friends.

I might not have liked George Robey but one comedian I

fell for was the sensational Bud Flanagan. Whilst I was with Henry we played Manchester's Palace Theatre for a week, and Flanagan and Allen shared the bill with us. Bud was the warmest, loveliest chap you could ever hope to meet. He really took a shine to me and we had a great week. After that, nearly every week, wherever I was performing, I'd receive a little note from him saying things like, 'We've just played the Edinburgh Empire, bloody awful audience but a great city.' When I hear his voice singing the theme tune to *Dad's Army* I get a little chill.

Another dear elderly comic was the talented Arthur Lucan. He was known as a character actor and had a world-famous act called 'Old Mother Riley', in which he dressed up as an old woman who bossed her daughter, Kitty, around. The act was the biggest thing in variety and he enjoyed a successful film career too. Kitty was played by Arthur's younger wife, Kitty McShane, and in reality their roles were swapped. She was a hard woman who browbeat the sweet old man until she ruined him. She had the biggest head and thought of herself as the star. Whenever I played with them in theatres I was always amazed to see she took the star dressing-room and he was forced up into the gods to get dressed with the chorus, carrying a deckchair under his arm.

Everyone in the business agreed that the three most unpopular women in the business were Kitty McShane, Beryl Formby and Nellie Driver, and I'll never forget the day all three came face to face. It was whilst we were recording a *Henry Hall Guest Night* at the Liverpool Empire. Kitty and Arthur were playing at the theatre and George Formby was a guest on our show. Mother was visiting me because we were so close to home, and Freda and I sat in the dressing-room listening to Kitty, Beryl and Mother lay into each other. All three had these huge reputations and were looking out for their own interests over billing. My word! It's a wonder the theatre didn't go up in flames! They screamed at each other and could well have gone for throats if Henry hadn't stepped in and separated them.

I met some wonderful artists during my years in the theatre and in radio but I never socialized with any of them as life was just so busy. We had a great time at the theatre but at the end of the week we'd go our own ways and hope, some day, to meet up again. It wasn't possible to build strong relationships. As a performer, I was unusual because I insisted that Freda had to be with me wherever I went. She was part of my outfit. We paid our own fares, unless we were with Henry: he knew how much she meant to me and put her down on paper as essential to my act.

Guest Night dominated my Thursdays throughout the war. No matter if we were appearing in standard variety shows or at a camp somewhere entertaining the troops, Thursday at seven thirty found us standing around microphones. Henry certainly kept me busy. When we weren't booked to appear in theatres, we would be on six-week compulsory ENSA tours and most Sundays we'd be entertaining wounded troops in hospitals or doing an extra concert at an airfield.

Getting to these troop bases was a right palaver. We'd travel on an Army truck, Henry, Freda, myself, the band and anyone else who was around, such as the wonderful impressionist Beryl Orde. Beryl was amusing company but she could be somewhat erratic. Henry and she were a combination to fill most people with horror. While Henry was a very proper Englishman, Beryl had a dangerous tongue and could easily go over the top. Her language was salty, but if you can't use swear words in the back of an Army truck where can you? She married Cyril Stapleton, the band leader. Anyway, there we'd be, driving around for about three hours even though we'd only be going a few miles: the reason for this was that they had to ensure we didn't know where we were going. Finding anywhere was hard work because many signposts and place names were removed or painted over to confuse any potential invader – or travelling artist! You'd follow an AA map, which would say things like 'turn left at the phone box on the right and turn right at the big hotel'. The trucks were so uncomfortable and made your bottom sore. They lurched around from side to side and we'd be in the back, hanging on and feeling sick.

We tended to rehearse all morning, do some sort of broadcast from two until four, then rehearse some more in time for another airing from eight until ten. Afterwards we were on a high and sleep was impossible, so Freda and I would meet up with some of the boys from the band and go out for the rest of the evening. We spent a great deal of time working in Weston-Super-Mare and after each show liked to walk down the front, all young people, linking arms, singing, with the bandsmen and the aircraft boys we'd befriended. We'd go to the Winter Gardens and have the last half-hour dancing. Then we'd go to a little café called Lou's. Lou was a fascinating woman, well educated and wealthy. She had a tiny café, little more than a hole, and she'd cook us whatever she had in, great plates of delicious sausages and chips, or even real eggs. She charged a pittance for it and there'd be loads of soldiers and RAF boys there. She looked upon it as her war work.

Apart from the bombs, the thing I hated most about the war was the blackout. As I said earlier, I've never liked the dark and had always slept with lights on. This was tricky during the war because if lights were on we had to have blackout curtains firmly pulled in place. It was all right in winter but during the summer I liked to sleep with the windows open and the curtains would blow and I'd be shining lights all over the place.

The worst thing was having to drive through the night, two hundred miles or more with little black caps on the headlights that only allowed the tiniest chink of light. It was horrible. All the traffic lights were fitted with blackout shields, so you could only just make out a small cross of light rather than the full circle. On foot it was dangerous too: even though council workers had painted white bands round lamp-posts and on the kerbs it was still easy to miss your footing. On one side there were Belisha beacons and pillar boxes to negotiate and on the other side sandbags against the shops. It was generally best to aim for the centre of the pavement.

Another thing about wartime was all the rationing. Because we were travelling we didn't have ordinary ration books as we couldn't register at shops. Instead, every Monday we had to go to the town hall wherever we were playing and queue for a weekly ration slip, which we'd then take to a shop. Every month everyone in the country was allowed supplementary rations, like jam and eggs, but we never got those and our rations were basic. We just had to rely on the kindness of the landlady and hope we didn't go hungry. We never had sweets unless I was presented with any on-stage.

In October 1941 the BBC contacted Henry to ask if he'd release me to appear in a radio play called *Sis Hopkins*. They were doing a series of hour-long broadcasts based on popular film musicals. The film *Sis Hopkins* had been a huge success and had starred Judy Canova, who had a singing voice that the BBC felt matched mine. At first Henry didn't want me to do it but they kept on at him so much that he agreed, on the condition that I was paid double my usual fee of fifteen guineas.

I was excited about the prospect because I loved plays and longed to do more serious acting. The play was to be rehearsed and recorded in Bangor so Freda and I travelled down, delighted to hear that Billy Tennent had been booked with his orchestra.

I had no idea what the play was about, just that we had three days to rehearse. Things didn't get off to a good start when we arrived and discovered that there were scripts but no music. I was then told by the producer that I was to sing ten numbers in the show. Now, to me, ten songs are enough to learn in three days when you have the music but here we were with no music and a script thick with dialogue. The producer – who I won't name – took us all to a cinema and showed us the film. Judy Canova was magnificent. As soon as the lights came up after the film Billy and I started kicking off, saying it was ridiculous for us to work without music. Billy's arranger was a wonderful chap called Alan Paul, and the only way for him to get the music was to sit through the film time after time after time, writing down the top line of the music as he heard it for every song.

I started to learn the tunes as best I could, then the producer dropped the bombshell that I had to play it all in a southern American drawl: the plot revolved around a farm girl who'd been discovered and launched as a big operatic star. It was a nightmare, and whilst Billy and I tried to get our heads round the music, the producer became hysterical and temperamental and we soon realized we hated each other. He was always screaming. By the end of the first day I was tearing my hair out. It was an impossible amount of work to dump on someone. Freda and I didn't sleep for three days. We spent all night under the bedclothes going through my songs and my accent. Freda was having operatic singing lessons at the time and had a terrific musical ear. She only had to hear something once and knew it. One of the ten songs was an operatic piece, from *Lakhmé*, a difficult aria to sing but luckily she knew it. She realized straight away that I wouldn't be able to sing it: it was for a coloratura and I wasn't even a soprano. So she taught one of the girls from the chorus to sing it and she pretended to be me. Freda then helped Alan Paul with the music, note for note, all the tunes he was stumbling over.

Half-way through the third day I threw a fit and refused to carry on. I packed my bags and stormed off to the station. It was the only time in my life that I'd refused to go on. The producer demanded that Freda went on in my place, pointing out she was the only one who knew the music. Freda was petrified and ran to the station to get me back. She told me she was going to be made to go on in my place and I wasn't having that. Somehow she talked me into returning and I did the play. The only way I could get through it, live on air and in front of a huge audience in the theatre, was to have Freda sitting on a stool facing me and Billy. She got us through the whole thing, conducting us for timing. I had to work with two music stands in front of me, one for my script and one for my music, keeping my eyes on both at the same time and having to turn pages quietly so they didn't rustle. It was the worst thing I've ever had to do but it was well received, a huge success – and I still don't know how we did it. At the end, when the audience applauded, Billy and I grabbed Freda and made her bow with us. I don't know who the audience thought she was! The producer was appalling and my agent, Lillian, reported him for making me a nervous wreck. I don't think he ever worked again in radio.

For those of us who continued to work in entertainment during the war, it became compulsory that we did six weeks work for ENSA each year. This allowed us to defer going into the services and meant that we'd receive orders from the ENSA offices in Drury Lane as to where we would be sent internationally to boost troop morale. We also did ENSA work in Britain when I'd sing novelty songs like 'We Mustn't Miss The Last Bus Home' and optimistic ballads like 'The World Will Sing Again'. I left the sob stuff to Vera Lynn. One run I'll never forget was when the band was stationed near Stonehenge, playing concerts in the big army camps in Larkhill and Bulford. We were to be in the area for a week so Henry settled Freda and me in a comfortable hotel in Amesbury. It was an old Elizabethan manor house and we were given the bridal suite, a beautiful oak-beamed room. We felt very grand staying there while Henry and the rest of the band roughed it elsewhere. At the time Freda and I travelled with a little Yorkshire terrier called Jem, and as soon as we unpacked our bags he started behaving strangely. To get to our bedroom we had to walk down the main corridor and he wouldn't go beyond a certain point. He'd stop and refuse to go any further on foot and had to be carried. This really baffled us, as did the discovery that none of the staff stayed overnight at the hotel. We soon found out why.

Every morning at three-thirty Jem would start to growl and stare at the door and his hair would be standing on end. It looked most peculiar as he had lovely long silky hair. Every time he growled we'd wake up and manage to calm him, but one night he growled more than usual and Freda woke with a start. She looked at the door and there stood this figure of a woman, with a horrible face, wearing a long, full grey dress. Well, Freda woke me up and pointed at the door and I saw her too, an ugly woman who just faded in front of our eyes. We were scared stiff. We pushed our beds together and spent the night lying there holding hands with the dog between us. The next night we were terrified in case she returned. She didn't, but we couldn't sleep anyway because there were loud noises directly overhead in the attics. It sounded as if someone was dragging something very heavy across the floor.

This sort of thing carried on all week and we were getting hardly any sleep. At the end of the week, Mother and Dad joined us for the weekend. On the Saturday night Mother went to the toilet in the early hours and heard scratching outside, as if someone was trying to get through the door to her. She was so frightened she stayed where she was for twenty minutes until Father went to look for her. She was so relieved to see him she fell at his feet in a dead faint and had to be carried back to bed. The next morning we went down to breakfast and everyone looked dreadful. No one had had a good night's sleep. No one wanted to talk about their experiences until a local man told us all about a lady, dressed in grey, who had lived in the house hundreds of years before and had murdered her lover in the attics. She had hanged herself in what had been our room from one of the beams. That was all I needed to hear. That day we packed and left.

About six weeks later, we heard that the owners had left the hotel because they couldn't take any more. The building had surrounded an enclosed cobbled courtyard, which had caved in, revealing a huge pit with tunnels running from it to Stonehenge. When specialists had investigated the tunnels they'd found skeletons of people who had been walled into alcoves along them. That was the first ghost I ever saw, and you can call me a damn fool if you like but I know what I saw, and what the two of us heard. I'd never known fear like it. Pure terror.

Ghost stories are commonplace in my profession and I've been in plenty of theatres that were meant to be haunted. Because I've been brought up in theatres, with old actors trying to scare me with tales of headless chorus girls roaming the stalls, supposedly haunted theatres never bothered me. I'd arrive at a new theatre and the stage manager would say, 'Don't be worried if you come down here when the stage is in darkness and you see someone walking across the boards. It's just the house ghost.' It was part of theatrical life, like greasepaint and band calls.

In variety I'd worked with plenty of animal acts and having seen some mistreating the animals I never thought

I'd have one of my own. I was a singer so there was no opening in my act for an animal anyway. At least, that's what I thought. Ever since I'd ridden around the airfield on Bess's back, I'd always loved dogs and when, in 1943, I heard that my hairdresser had a poodle he didn't want I was determined to buy it. I paid him twenty-five pounds and was stunned when he gave me this nervous ball of fluff. Freda helped me clip it, and when we got rid of all the matted fur that was weighing her down we found she was only six inches high. I called her Mitzi and couldn't bear to be apart from her so she joined Freda and me at the theatre each night. I left her in the dressing-room when I went on. One night someone let her out, and she followed the sound of my voice and trotted out on to the stage. The audience thought it was part of the act and aahhed. I was singing 'I Only Have Eyes For You' on a dimly-lit stage, very sophisticated and romantic, and the audience were laughing. I thought, Have my knickers fallen down? I stopped singing, saw Mitzi and picked her up. She sat on my shoulder, licking my ear, whilst I carried on singing. When I got to a particularly high note I was amazed when she joined in, yawning. It brought the house down and after that she became part of my act. Each night she'd come on with me and sit on my shoulder whilst I sang. Every time I hit the high note she yawned.

Not everyone in the audience thought it was as sweet as I did. Once, when I was playing the Sunderland Empire, I went to the bank and was accosted by the manager. He came out of his office, into the bank and said, 'I'm going to report you for cruelty towards that little dog.' I couldn't believe it. He went on, 'I know how you make her yawn. You stick a pin into her bottom.' I was indignant and adamant that I didn't so he demanded to see my nails and as they were long said I must dig them into her to make her yawn. The only way I could prove him wrong was to set Mitzi down on the bank counter and sing right there and then, in front of everyone. And when I hit that note she yawned. He could see I wasn't hurting her and apologized but he made me feel so rotten – that anyone could think I'd be cruel to an animal! Frequently people would ask me how I made Mitzi yawn like that. They just couldn't understand that it was nothing to do with me. She just did it.

I've never mistreated an animal but I won't forget a variety act who did. The woman's name was Korringa. She had two Czechoslovakian assistants, who would lay paving stones on her chest then break them into tiny pieces. Sometimes it would take seven or eight hits with a mallet to break them. She had a speciality act with snakes and crocodiles. I am terrified of crocodiles and kept out of her way as much as possible. We played the Blackpool Palace together, and each night I had to get from one side of the stage to the other, around the back, and had to pass these long glass coffins containing the crocodiles, all lit up to keep them warm. I'd have palpitations walking past them, watching them watching me. Korringa used to put her head in their mouths and it wasn't until afterwards that I discovered they were harmless because she'd had all their teeth pulled out. Those poor creatures. One day the stage manager knocked on my door and said, 'Don't come out, one of the crocodiles is loose.' I didn't need telling twice! Towards the end of the war somebody electrocuted all the crocodiles in their tanks because it was thought Korringa was 'not on our side'.

I'm glad to say that if anyone in the theatre saw animals being mistreated the owners were usually reported to the authorities. Some trainers would beat their animals or prod them with sticks that gave off electric shocks, that sort of thing. Mother wasn't an animal lover but if she saw cruelty she reported it straight away.

CHAPTER TEN

Breakdown

Everything in my world was wonderful. I was touring the country with Henry and our radio broadcasts achieved rave reviews. I was financially stable and able to put down some roots, renting a flat on Tottenham Court Road in London, near Goodge Street station. In those days it was a fabulous area, richly cosmopolitan and full of artists and theatricals. Soho was just round the corner and the streets buzzed with life at the markets and shops. It was the first home I'd known since leaving Manchester when I was twelve. For Freda and me it stood for much more than just a base when in town: it was home and gave us security.

The flat belonged to a Belgian who had been in the Folies Bergère, an exotic woman called Madame Faley. She had furnished the house with beautiful continental furniture, and lots of Spanish shawls were draped everywhere. The flat was six floors up and overlooked the whole of London. When the sirens went off Freda and I would stand at the window to watch the planes coming and see the big guns shooting them out of the sky. Some of the German planes would get through our defences and if it looked as though they were heading our way we'd go and stand near the lift shaft as that was the safest part of the building. Neither Freda nor I used the shelters regularly but on occasion, if we were out in a raid, we'd be forced down into one and sometimes ended up huddled on an underground platform. Down there someone would start a song and I'd sing to the crowds.

Having just settled ourselves in London I had no idea that I would spend six months of 1943 in Manchester, as a virtual prisoner in my parents' house. It all started with the return of the blackouts that had caused me to suffer from stage fright a few years earlier. As before, these blackouts occurred whilst I was performing, although thankfully never during a broadcast. Henry would be conducting, the band playing and all would be swinging until I suddenly dried. Henry would glance at me anxiously and the boys would belt out on their instruments to cover for me whilst I sank into a chair. I attempted to shrug off the attacks but Henry insisted I saw a doctor, who advised me to take a break. He pointed out that for two and a half years I hadn't taken so much as a day off: weekdays I performed with Henry and each Sunday I'd be singing to wounded troops in hospitals. Henry and Freda ganged up on me, and reluctantly I agreed to say goodbye to the band. To escape the bombing, Freda took me back to Manchester, where it had ceased. When we got home Mother was furious with me for agreeing to rest, because if I wasn't working I wasn't earning. It was too much. I had a major nervous breakdown. Only Freda cared what happened to me and she became my nurse. All my confidence had left me and I used to sit in a chair all day, frightened to leave the house or of not being near Freda. I stopped eating and caring for myself. I just didn't want to exist any more. Mother eventually tired of haranguing me and decided to ignore me. For six months I refused to leave the house. I can't explain my state of mind at that time: it was as if I was living inside a long dark tunnel and there was no sign of light at the end.

Freda never left my side: she lived every painful second with me. In the end she decided that the only way I was going to get better was if she pushed me into it. Very slowly she got me to face the outside world. First she stunned me by announcing that I was going to stand at the open front door. I refused and dug myself into my chair, but she persisted and told me to trust her. The walk to the front door was terrifying, far worse than going on-stage. Each step seemed to take for ever, as if my feet had turned to lead. I was shaking and perspiring. Oh, it was awful. When I reached it, she opened the door and I saw the familiar garden, the people walking past, and I took deep breaths of air. For the next week we repeated the experience and by the weekend I found I was looking forward to my trip to the door.

The following week Freda worked on getting me to stand just outside the door, clinging to the door-frame for dear life. Then, a little while later, she walked me into the garden, then to the garden gate, and so on. Mother shook her head and thought all I needed was a good smack around the face to cure me.

Henry was very concerned and started to plot with Freda about getting me back on-stage. He came to Manchester one week, performing at the Palace Theatre, and arranged to take me to lunch at the Midland Hotel. I took a lot of persuading to go but felt I would be all right if Freda was with me. She helped me into my best clothes and steered me into the taxi, but then broke the news that she wasn't going with me. I tried to get out of the car but she refused to let me, saying I'd be fine and that I needed to prove to Henry and myself that I could do this; that I could venture out into the world again. I was a wreck during the ride into the city centre, and when we pulled up outside the hotel I was so relieved to see the familiar shape of Henry waiting for me that when he opened the taxi door I nearly fell into his arms. He put his arm around me and held me tight as he steered me through the lobby and into the restaurant.

He found us a corner table, and sat me with my back to the majority of the room. He didn't give me time to think, just told me all the news about the band. I was fine until half-way through the meal, when I started to cry and said I had to go home. I had beads of perspiration running down my face and felt as if everyone in the room was staring at me. He understood and we took a taxi back to Freda. I was a wreck but mentally I'd crossed a threshold and after that excursion we started to venture further afield than the garden gate.

Shortly after our abandoned lunch, Henry invited Freda and me to visit him when he was playing at the Nottingham Empire. We were to watch the band from the wings and I found I was actually looking forward to hearing the music again and smelling the unique smell of the theatre: a mix of sawdust and greasepaint. Freda dressed us both in beautiful evening gowns and I stood there listening to the wonderful band, my foot tapping. I even managed to give Freda a smile. Of course, I had no idea that she and Henry had been plotting. That was until I heard him suddenly speaking to the audience, saying, 'You all remember an artist called Betty Driver, I'm sure. Well, she's been ill but she's here tonight so would you give her a big welcome.' I was horrified and looked around for the nearest exit but Freda blocked my path and firmly pushed me on to the stage. I stumbled on in tears, looked at Henry and he was in tears. I glanced back at Freda and she was bawling her eyes out! Henry grasped my hand and gave it a squeeze, then said that he was going to play one of our old numbers and suggested we sang it together. That took him a lot of guts because he was tone-deaf and had a terrible voice. I didn't want to let him down, or the audience who kept cheering me on, so the pianist started, the band picked up and we started to sing. He held my hand and faced me, encouraging me, singing straight at me, as if the audience didn't exist. Gradually he let go of my hands and eased back towards the band to conduct them whilst I carried on singing.

I went right through the song, did an encore, came off the stage and fainted into Freda's arms. I had returned to the stage, and from that moment my nerves settled and I returned to normality. I'm thrilled to say that the blackouts have never returned. Of course, in those days, celebrities weren't bothered by the press as they are today. No one knew I'd been ill. When I returned to the business after my six-month break I was shocked to discover that everyone thought I'd had the time off to have a baby. They'd ask if I'd had a boy or a girl. I was so indignant!

With my confidence restored, my agent booked me to appear in a ten-month revue at London's Coliseum called *Foolish But It's Fun*, a big West End show packed with sketches and songs. The bill was topped by Nervo and Knox, an elderly comedy double-act, who had become famous as part of the Crazy Gang, a group of six gents of a certain age who made films and were the Queen's favourite entertainers. Having fallen for Bud Flanagan I was looking forward to working with two other members of this world-famous act. It took me no longer than the first week of rehearsals to size them up and a bigger pair of swine never lived! They were practical jokers, and very jealous of any other act who went down well with the audience. I remember that the only time my father ever stood backstage to watch me perform was when I was in this show. It was the opening night and the Duchess of Kent was in the audience. I had on a beautiful gown and was just about to make my entrance when Jimmy Nervo came behind me and unzipped my frock, which fell off in full view of the audience. I pulled myself together and started to sing. Half-way through a lovely ballad, Nervo walked on-stage with a bucket and shouted, 'I'm just going to make the beds.' I was trying to do a sophisticated act! Then from the other side Teddy Knox came on, picked up the microphone I was using and walked off-stage with it. The audience thought it was part of the act and laughed, but I found it really upsetting. Thankfully I had a strong voice and didn't need a microphone anyway. My dad saw what was going on and threatened to thump them so they brought back the microphone and I finished my act. Jealousy, that's all it was. My act went down too well for their liking.

My agent, Morris Aza, had similar problems with their tricks. He had worked as a clapperboard boy on a Crazy Gang movie, but while he was away from the set they nailed his board shut. When the director called, 'Action!' he couldn't get it open and was shouted at. He didn't like them either.

My dressing room was next to theirs and only accessed by a little flight of stairs beside the stage door. Once I was coming down the stairs as Teddy Knox was going up. As I went past he put out his foot and I went flying straight down the stairs, ripped all the tendons in my foot and was off for a fortnight.

He never apologized but I suppose I should be grateful they never did their ball-bearing trick on me. Anne Ziegler wasn't so fortunate. She was a beautiful woman with a fantastic voice and had a semi-operatic singing act with her partner Webster Booth. Audiences adored them, which meant, of course, that Nervo and Knox despised them. During one performance the comics climbed up above the stage and sat on the lighting rig whilst Webster and Anne were singing. Half-way through the act, Nervo and Knox dropped a load of ball-bearings on to the stage. Anne was in the middle of a wonderful piece, wandering about the stage as she sang. She didn't see the ball-bearings and slipped on them, falling flat on her back, crinoline going everywhere. The fall hurt her badly and she couldn't move. Nervo and Knox were awful, petty people and hated the dainty Anne because she was classical. After her fall she had to wear a steel corset for the rest of the run because her back had been damaged.

At the time Freda was having Italian singing lessons, and Webster heard her practising in the dressing room. He asked Freda to go on in Anne's place, saying that the dresses would fit her. Freda was quite taken with the idea but very nervous. In the meantime Anne heard he'd asked her and she said to him, 'If that kid wears my clothes and goes on in my place I'll leave you!' So that scotched Freda!

Whilst I was at the Coliseum, Freda and I were instructed in the art of fire-watching. Each night, after the show, everyone at the theatre had to take it in turns to stand on the roof and put out any fires caused by the bombing. Freda and I pulled the short straw and ended up teamed with Nervo and Knox for fire-watching duty. We were shown how to use stirrup pumps and given tin helmets. It all seemed very exciting and both Freda and I were looking forward to dealing with any incendiary bombs that came our way.

Underneath the stage at the Coliseum, there was a sub-basement, which was used as an air-raid shelter: when we were on duty we'd sleep in it until the sirens went off. It was homely down there, with bunks and a kettle for brewing up. The first night we were on duty the sirens went off and we grabbed our tin hats, but Nervo and Knox decided they didn't want us joining in, locked us in the shelter and wouldn't let us out. They had a hell of a time that night because they were undermanned and the bombs kept dropping. One went right through the glass dome on top of the theatre and landed in the orchestra pit on the drum kit. Another fell on to the revolving stage and started a fire immediately above us in the shelter and we couldn't get out to help. I was furious, but when it happened a second night Freda and I resigned our posts, saying sulkily that we weren't playing any more.

It wasn't all doom and gloom at the Coliseum: there was a handsome Irish singer in the show called Patrick McGraw, who became my boyfriend. He was a lovely man and always wore a little finger ring. I admired it and he gave it to me as a token. We started to go out together. It was all very innocent and I enjoyed an almost teenage-like crush on him. We hadn't been seeing each other for long when my mother came on a visit. The first thing she did when she was alone in my dressing room was to go through my handbag. Of course, she found the ring. She was furious and called me a tart and a trollop. She was so vicious that I burst into tears. Freda was outraged and bundled her off back to Manchester on the next train. Shortly afterwards she had to go into hospital and Freda and I spent our Sundays faithfully travelling up to Manchester to spend an hour with her at visiting time. She'd sit up in bed, surrounded by pillows and speak over me as if I weren't there, asking Freda, 'Who's she been out tarting with then?' I don't know what she thought I was getting up to. Whatever it was, it wasn't happening. I was too frightened for a start. She'd seen to that when I was twelve and she had told me the facts of life.

During the run at the Coliseum I continued to make radio broadcasts around London. For six weeks running I appeared in a radio show, *Yankee Doodle Doo*, which was recorded at the Paris cinema, a lovely theatre in the West End. I shared the bill with two wonderful comedians, an Austrian called Vic Oliver and Ben Lyons, who normally performed a sophisticated double act with his wife Bebe Daniels. Vic always dressed in tails and played the violin as well as cracking jokes. He was something of a womanizer, who went on to marry Winston Churchill's daughter Sarah. When I first met him he was all smarmy, trying it on, but I ignored him so he announced that I was too big for him and turned his attention to Freda. He introduced himself to her and asked her age. She said she was eighteen at which he said, 'I prefer my girls a bit younger. I like them about sixteen, but for you I'll overlook your age.' Freda called him a dirty old man and stayed out of his way after that. Despite all that Vic's gags always made me laugh.

Each week we had a different guest, like Rex Harrison or Evelyn Laye, but the one who caused us the most excitement was Bob Hope. When we were told he was going to join us I was thrilled: I loved his films. We rehearsed the show in the afternoon without him, and he arrived at the back of the theatre in a big camel coat, accompanied by a singer called Frances Langford, who had done a great deal of work with Glenn Miller. Following on behind was this huge entourage of men all clutching briefcases. His party filled the theatre aisle and he walked on to the stage and seemed to fill the whole auditorium with his presence. He said such charming things to us and refused a rehearsal, saying it wasn't necessary.

That night I stood at the side of the stage with Ben Lyons and watched him at work. I'd never seen anything like it: repartee so fast it wasn't true. He 'felt' the audience and picked up on how they were reacting to his jokes. Seated each side of the stage were two of his men and there were more in the audience: when he felt a gag hadn't gone down very well he'd glance towards one of these men who'd call back 'sixty-three' or 'three-oh-three' and Bob would launch into another. At the end of the show I asked one of these men what they were doing and he said Bob had the biggest gag library in the world and had memorized them all. The men were his gag writers and just by calling out the number of the joke Bob would know which one they meant. Incredible.

The West End was a fascinating place to be during the war, filled with colourful characters: theatricals, Pearly Kings, Italian café owners, market-stall holders, barrow boys, a rainbow of coloured uniforms. We performers made every effort to join in the war effort. Actresses like Evelyn Laye and Cicely Courtneidge threw lavish parties to entertain the troops and take their minds off their troubles: so many were apart from their families and loved ones for so long. Cicely was married to Jack Hulbert and they did a sophisticated double act. They were very fine singers and dancers. Throughout the whole of the war Jack Hulbert served as a special constable. He'd be in a show at night then during the day would patrol the streets as a special. Of course, everyone knew him because he and Cicely had made a number of films together, and it was a tremendous boost to Londoners to see him involved with the war effort. At the end of the war Cicely was one of the stars of a concert at the Royal Albert Hall to mark the standing down of the Home Guard and had the honour of giving the official order to 'Stand down, gentlemen.' She was a close friend of Jimmy Nervo and called at the Coliseum to see him. Then she always sought out Freda and me. She was a lovely lady, very classy. I could never understand why she was so matey with Jimmy Nervo.

Our lives in London were dominated by routine. After shows at the Coliseum Freda and I often wandered down to Tottenham Court Road to a theatrical boarding-house called Olivelli's, run by an extended Italian family. It was made up of three large terraces, which had been knocked into one. It was the favourite place to get digs in London but you didn't have to stay there to enjoy its wonderful hospitality. In the basement Mrs Olivelli had a huge kitchen, which boasted the biggest table I've ever seen in my life, about twenty foot long. It dominated the room, along with a big black cooking range and an upright piano. She'd always have great big pans of minestrone going, bread and butter beans. After the show at night, we'd go back there and it would be full of artists. We all met up there, snug together around the table, deep beneath London. The place would be brimming over with stars, all tucking into Mrs Olivelli's wonderful food. We'd sit there eating and suddenly someone would say, 'What do you think of this number?' and they'd sit at the piano and start singing to us. Perhaps Max Miller would try out a new gag, or a couple of American dancers would climb on to the table and go through a new routine. It was fantastic. Freda and I went there from the Coliseum every Saturday night. The atmosphere was electric, like a film set.

I was always bumping into Max Miller during the war. He seemed to be forever walking up and down Charing Cross Road where all the out-of-work pros used to hang about, meeting up with each other. Max wouldn't be out of work, he'd be there because he knew that some of the pros had something he could buy – their gags. He would accost out-of-work variety artists and buy gags off them for a paltry amount, usually sixpence. If he gave half a crown it was for a show-stopper, and that's how he got his act. He never wrote anything himself. I'd watch him through my agent's window, upstairs, as he'd huddle in a shop doorway and listen to gag after gag. One man told me he thought he'd given him half his act.

Another place we'd go to eat was a cabbies' café called

Gold's. It was on Little Denmark Street where the music publishers were, a tiny place run by a Jewish family. It was very basic yet homely, with oilcloth on the table and wooden benches. All the pros went there for lunch and sat side by side with the taxi drivers.

I was still in contact with Henry Hall, and whenever he was working in London he'd call on me and beg me to come back to him. Having been booked at the Coliseum for ten months I couldn't just drop everything but I agreed happily that, when the run ended, I would go back. Even after we'd established my return, Henry continued to call on us. He was such a lovely man and would often ask Freda to go into town with him to choose flowers or jewellery for his wife. There he'd be, this middle-aged man, linking arms with a seventeen-year-old girl and walking her around London. One day, in the Charing Cross Road, another band leader, Louis Leavey, stopped them, winked and said Henry was a dark horse. Poor Henry didn't understand, and Freda had to point out that people had jumped to the conclusion that she was his girlfriend. He was appalled.

As I've said, as well as performing in the revue, I was not neglecting my radio work. During the war years I appeared in countless programmes, often running to theatres to record two or three numbers whenever I had a spare after-noon. One of my favourites was *Shipmates Ashore*, which was recorded at the London Merchant Navy Club and was hosted by Doris Hare. The show would start each week with the announcer declaring, 'A meeting place in the heart of London for men of the Merchant Service. Call in or tune in for music, dancing, refreshments and a friendly welcome by your chief stewardess, Doris Hare.'

Doris and I got on well together and became friends, little knowing that in 1969 we would start together in *Coronation Street* before she became world-famous as Mum in the comedy show *On The Buses*. During the forties Doris was a huge star, of theatre as well as radio. She'd worked with everyone and everyone adored her. Whenever she performed in Manchester she stayed in theatrical digs in Daisy Avenue run by a woman called Alma McKee. It was a huge house divided into two: one side was for serious actors, the other for variety and Alma never let the two mix. Doris would be appearing in a big play in town so she was always in the best dining-room, but I was allowed to visit and eat with her, although I should have been in the other, shabbier one with the variety crowd.

Alma was a real character, a large woman and an immense gossip. She'd say, 'I had so-and-so in here last week and, ooooh, if I could open my mouth I'd ruin his career!' During one meal I had there with Doris, Alma stood between us the entire time gossiping about the pros she'd had staying with her. 'He's a dirty swine,' and 'If her husband knew what she got up to!' All through the meal Doris and I kept glancing at each other, trying not to laugh. After the war Doris was awarded the MBE for her services to the Merchant Navy. *Shipmates Ashore* was a wonderful programme and carried on running even after the war ended.

Another show we all did, which ran well into the late 1940s, was *Worker's Playtime*. These shows were based on the idea that the factories were full of men and women who worked twelve-hour shifts in munitions, producing guns and machinery. They needed to be entertained but didn't have time for fun outside working hours, so the shows came to them, playing in their canteens. Each show was recorded and broadcast at lunchtime in factories all around the country. I loved doing those shows, standing on a makeshift stage and getting everyone to sing along whilst they munched their sandwiches. We also did *Midnight Worker's Playtime* for the night shift.

Garrison Theatre was a weekly radio show broadcast from the Shepherd's Bush Empire. The show was meant to sound as if it came live from an Army barracks, the orchestra was made up of men from the RAF band and, where possible, troops made up the audience. Jack Warner was a regular on the show, playing the part of a Cockney soldier who was always making daft remarks and interrupting things. Of course, most people remember him in the title role of television's *Dixon of Dock Green*, the gentle police series that ran from 1955 to 1976. I only did a handful of *Garrison Theatre* shows but I can remember being more enamoured of Jack than of his sisters Elsie and Doris Waters.

When the run of *Foolish But It's Fun* ended in 1944, I did a couple of weeks' touring before starting up again with Henry Hall. One of those weeks found me in Chatham. Freda and I stayed in digs as it was too far to travel back to our Tottenham Court Road flat at night. Also London had suddenly become a dangerous place again, due to the arrival of the flying bombs. The landlady in Chatham said to us, 'Don't be frightened in the night because all the doodle-bugs fly over on their way to London. None ever fall on us.' In the fields around Chatham were the guns that would try to shoot them down. On the first night we saw all these flying bombs with their tails on fire, on their way to fall, unannounced, upon the heads of Londoners. It was a sinister and frightening sight. Also, we knew that as long as we could hear a doodlebug's engine we were safe. When it cut out though . . .

The theatre I was playing at was on the river's edge and my dressing-room, which opened out on to the backstage area, had a window that offered a fabulous view of the water. All was fine until the Wednesday matinée. I was on-stage singing 'For All We Know, We May Never Meet Again' and Freda was in the dressing-room when she saw a flying bomb heading towards us. She threw open the dressing-room door and frantically waved at the stage manager. Because the show had to carry on he told Freda to stand at the window and report on how near it was getting. As usual she collected our handbags, then stood there watching this doodlebug as it came closer and closer. As it flew over the theatre my microphone started to shake and the audience stood up. Then the engine cut out and we all froze, waiting. Amazingly the wind caught the bomb and blew it over the theatre, towards the river. It exploded on a tiny island. Then I carried on singing!

I returned to Henry after a break of more than a year, and it felt as if I was coming home. It was marvellous to be with him and the boys in the band again. By this stage many theatres had been damaged by bombs so he booked us into cinemas for a few days, to give performances between films and record *Guest Night* on Thursday evening. Once we were appearing at a cinema in Canterbury and we befriended some American servicemen. The well-fitting, tan uniforms of the Americans had been a regular sight in London since 1942, but I'd never really taken the time to get to know them. The crowd in Canterbury that we met were nice lads and after we parted company they wrote to us and sent us presents. I was friendly with one, called Carl Fisher, until suddenly his letters stopped and I was told he'd been killed. Then, just over a year ago, he telephoned me at Granada – fifty-five years later – and said he was in England and wanted to meet up. I arranged for him to call at my apartment, thinking it would be wonderful to see an old pal.

When he arrived I rushed to answer the doorbell but instead of the tall, bronzed soldier I remembered there was a little old man I didn't recognize at all. He came in and started to reminisce about Canterbury, but his memories didn't quite tally with mine or Freda's. He was adamant that we'd been more than friends and that we'd spent one night together in a sleeping-bag. He said, 'You said to me, "It's no use you trying anything on, I'm a virgin." ' Freda and I stared at him and didn't know what to say. For one thing I would never have got into a sleeping-bag with a man and said such a thing and for another Freda never left my side. Then he said I'd taken him to meet my mother and that there had been an understanding between us. He asked if we were going to spend any of the evening alone together. All the time I kept glancing at Freda, signalling her not to leave me alone with him. In the end we got him out of the apartment and took him for dinner at the local hotel. He kept going on and on about how close we'd been and Freda and I exchanged horrified looks. Alex Ferguson, the Manchester United manager, was at the next table, killing himself laughing at my expression. Eventually we got rid of him and I've no idea who he thought I was.

Towards the end of the war I recognized the tell-tale signs that my nerves were starting to fail me again. I feared

I was going to have another breakdown. One week we were playing the Birmingham Hippodrome and Henry called a doctor in to see me. He put me on some tablets and told me to take a couple of weeks off work. Both Henry and I hoped a fortnight would be enough to put me right as we'd been booked on an ENSA tour of France, Belgium, Holland and Germany. The doctor was pleased to hear this, and told Henry to get as much champagne down me as possible as the bubbles would help cure my nerves. I didn't like this idea because I didn't drink alcohol: watching my father downing it all my life had put me right off it. The doctor, however, insisted that it would help, and said I had to drink at least four glasses a day! Now, that would be most people's idea of heaven, but I was anguished at the prospect.

ENSA had been set up in 1939 by the Government, as the Entertainment National Service Association, and was run by theatre director Basil Dean, who was given the brief of co-ordinating theatrical talent to entertain the troops overseas. The first ENSA concert had been given in November 1939, in France, and starred Gracie Fields. All actors and musicians, who had been allowed to remain in civvies, were booked for six weeks' compulsory ENSA work each year. This European tour was to be my first experience of working overseas and I was excited. Freda wouldn't come abroad with me because we had to have injections and she had a phobia about them. We had to go to this hospital for foreign diseases on the Embankment in London for them and I remember the embarrassment I caused the poor young doctor. Because I wore strapless dresses in my act I refused to have the injections in my arm in case they left blotches and insisted that I'd have them in my thigh. His hand shook as I lifted my skirt up!

We set off for France in khaki. Henry was a major and I was a captain, with pips on my shoulder and a very dashing uniform. I was sad to leave Freda in England but looking forward to what I considered an adventure. It was my first time abroad, and what a place to start! The beautiful city of Paris, which had only recently been liberated. After years of staring at bombed wrecks of cities it was sheer joy to see Parisian architecture. Our first performance in Paris was at a theatre on the Champs Elysées, to a packed audience of servicemen. They were even hanging off the light fittings. When we arrived at the theatre Henry put a bottle of champagne on my dressing table, but I refused to touch it. The first number I did that night was a new one called 'Don't Fence Me In'. The audience was warm and appreciative but when I looked out over the footlights all I could see was khaki and Air Force blue. When I'd finishing singing I was astounded by the applause that rang around the auditorium: I'd never had such an ovation in my life.

After the show I was on a natural high and Henry forced me to have a sip of champagne when I got back to my dressing-room, then another after dinner later that night. We were staying at an enormous hotel, along with other famous orchestras such as Eric Winston's and Ambrose's. It was May, and I'll never forget the lilies of the valley that surrounded the hotel, thousands of them. Henry had some picked and placed in a bowl in my bedroom. The chestnut trees were in blossom and the air was fragrant. It was the best time of year to see Paris.

The next day Henry took me to the Palace of Versailles

where there was a glorious champagne bar where they sold iced champagne, poured over tall pyramids of flute glasses. Everywhere we went Henry ordered champagne. He was teetotal, as I was, but as I was so reluctant to drink what the doctor had ordered he agreed to match me sip for sip. After a glass and walking in the heat I felt light-headed, but back at the theatre another glass was waiting for me in my dressing-room. The performance went well again and afterwards Henry announced he was taking me to a little club where we could dance and have more champagne. This was unheard-of: Henry had two left feet and we ended up walking around the dance floor in time to the music. I loved ballroom dancing and normally can't abide bad dancers as partners but I adored Henry so I was happy just to be close to him and try to avoid his feet treading on mine. By this time my little sips of champagne had turned into full glasses. I had no idea how potent it was and started to get a liking for it. We ate and drank, danced and drank, then left the club through a revolving door. We walked out and the air hit us, the champagne hit us, and we both sank down to the pavement and sat on the edge of the kerb whilst the street spun around us. We couldn't move. That was my introduction to champagne, and from then on if ever I had bad nerves I reached for the champagne bottle!

I had never made a conscious decision not to drink. Probably I didn't have time to start, I was always so busy. A lot of variety artists had drink-related problems and it might have been that seeing them made me wary of alcohol. My father was a heavy drinker – going to the pub was his only escape from my mother. He drank beer, pint after pint, and it never seemed to affect him. He was also a chain-smoker but I've never smoked either, so perhaps I was reacting against him. But don't get me wrong: I wasn't a paragon of virtue!

Although I was in France as a captain and had to wear khaki all day, I had brought with me two beautiful gowns that Freda had run up on the Singer. In Paris Henry took me to a reception in a château whose interior had been designed by Norman Hartnell. The reception was thrown in Norman's honour, and at one point his lady came up to me, said she'd seen the show and admired my dresses. She asked me who my designer was. I said, 'My sister made them.' She was very interested, thinking Freda was someone she should have heard of. Her face was a picture when I told her, 'We travel with a little hand machine and Freda cuts out the material on the dressing-room floor.'

During that European tour we followed a circuit, appearing in theatres immediately after a troupe of actors performing in a comedy play. One of those actors was Margot Bryant, who later became a great friend when I joined *Coronation Street* where she was a favourite as cat-loving Minnie Caldwell. Margot had appeared in the West End as a flapper in the 1920s, dancing in the chorus whilst Fred and Adele Astaire took centre stage in *Stop Flirting*. I hardly saw anything of her during the 1945 tour and was so pleased I had the chance to get to know her better during my first seven years on the *Street*. Like many of the original cast she was a real old trouper.

When the war finally ended, we were in Eindhoven, Holland. That day we'd been given a tour of the Philips factory, where all the radios and television sets were made, and that evening we did our show. Suddenly while we were on the stage sirens went off, whistles were blown, hooters sounded, bells rang and the stage manager rushed on-stage and shouted 'The war's over!' The place erupted. The audience surged out on to the streets and we followed. All that night we marched around Eindhoven, carrying torches and candles, singing. Bells were ringing and everyone opened their windows and put all their lights on. Even street lights came on and searchlights criss-crossed the sky. The brightness surprised me – it was magical. After putting up with the blackout for so many years, we had begun to feel it would never be bright again. That night we partied for hours. The relief that it was finally over was indescribable. The only blot on the celebrations for me was that Freda wasn't with me. We'd been right through the war together but because of her fear of needles she had remained in England and saw in VE Day in Manchester.

The European tour ended with a week in Germany, and we played our last concert at an Army camp, which was the last place the lads went to before they were allowed home. It was a delousing centre and we were booked to entertain thousands, all crowded together in a hall. The commanding officer came to see us before the show and said, 'Don't be frightened when you go on to the stage and look out into the audience. All you'll see will be ghostly faces.' He explained that these poor lads had been covered from head to toe in delousing powder and looked as if they'd been dipped into flour bags. I felt so sorry for them: they'd been fighting for months then had to suffer such degrading treatment. The band went on, played until the intermission and died a death. There was no applause, no singing along. Nothing. Then we realized that these lads had been fighting for so long that they didn't know the tunes we were playing. During the interval we rushed about rigging up old songs.

The band started to busk and luckily I knew the songs. I went on in a gorgeous evening dress and sang the first song, but still there was nothing, no response at all. They just sat staring at us, exhausted. I couldn't bear to see them so dejected, it tore at my heart, so I suggested to Henry that I should move off the stage and walk into the audience. The song was 'You Made Me Love You' and I found a young boy sitting near the front. Tears were streaming down his cheeks, leaving lines in the white powder. I moved over to him, sat on his knee and put my arms round him, ignoring his concern that the powder would rub off on me. I sang to him until I made him smile then moved on to the next lad, and so on. I moved right through the audience, getting these boys to sing along with me. They were crying, I was crying. Eventually the organizers pushed away some of the chairs and I started to dance with the lads whilst singing to them. It was the most moving experience of my life, and to this day I still get letters from men who were at that delousing camp.

While we were in Germany we were taken to the Arnhem bridge, which had been demolished. The battle of Arnhem had been airborne and was Montgomery's only major defeat. Three divisions of paratroops and gliders were dropped behind German lines but few reached the bridge. We were rowed across the Rhine and looked after by an officer called Roy Spear, whose brother Eric later wrote the theme tune to *Coronation Street*. We went into Arnhem and Roy showed us a hill that was actually a pile of dead bodies. Standing on top was a big boxer dog with cropped ears. I don't know who the people in the pile were but it was an indescribable sight that I cannot forget. That same week we were taken to Belsen, which had only just been liberated. The stench that greeted us when we came into the surrounding area is another thing that haunts me still and I get very upset when people who lived nearby during the war years insist that they didn't know what the camp was used for. The smell of burnt flesh and hair must constantly have been in the air. I'm glad I experienced it, because although the memories are painful, things like that should never be forgotten.

I know it probably sounds an odd thing to say, but in some ways I was sad to see the end of the war. Everything had seemed exciting: we lived for each moment and I was proud to have helped in keeping morale up. When it was over, life became terribly, terribly dull.

CHAPTER ELEVEN

The Biggest Mistake of My Life

The war was over but as a member of ENSA I was still in uniform. As the troops slowly returned to Britain they still needed entertaining, still had spirits that needed lifting. I eventually set foot in peacetime England just a few days after VE Day and, needless to say, it was straight back to work, touring with Henry around the country and broadcasting *Guest Night* each Thursday, week in, week out. This carried on for two and a half years after the war. I was happy doing it, felt safe in the routine and comfortable in the company of the band – they had become my family and I drew confidence from them – but it couldn't last for ever. It was Mother, raising her voice in Manchester, who put an end to the happiest period of my life. Someone had suggested to her that I was too dependent on the band and Henry, and that it was preventing me moving on. This was true but I enjoyed it and was horrified when Mother asked my agent to find me other work. As he agreed with her I was forced to give the idea serious consideration. Even Freda had to admit that Mother had a point, and there was no telling where my career would lead me if I was given freedom to allow it wings.

Henry took my departure badly: he looked on me as a daughter and we'd been through so much together. However, he didn't try to stop me, knowing it was the best career move I could make. The BBC stopped *Guest Night* because it was felt it wouldn't be so popular without my spot. Henry tried to continue with other singers but they never worked out and shortly after I left him he retired, in 1948. He was the most fantastic man to work with and I owe him so much. In his autobiography, Henry said a kind thing about me: 'She could follow anyone on the bill – again the triumph of personality which I am so certain is the greatest single factor in the making of a star.' When you consider that Mother never gave me any praise at all and the best Dad could manage was that I was 'all right', I really treasure what Henry said next: 'She was a performer of whom it could be said, truthfully for once, that she was completely different on-stage. Off-stage she was shy and quiet and looked and spoke like a real Lancashire girl. On-stage vitality cracked in her every movement and personality swept over the footlights.' Henry was a true friend and when he died, about fifteen years ago, I was grief-stricken for days. About three days before his death we spoke on the phone and he said, 'They were great times, weren't they?' He was right – they *were* great times. He was the one man in my life I totally adored. I had a huge crush on him but it never developed into anything: he was a married man and his family was part of my life. Losing him was like losing a father.

I was in a fortunate position when I left Henry Hall because bookings flooded in and I could choose what I wanted to do. It was only after I'd left the band that I realized just how little Henry had been paying me. Mother and my agent both agreed that I could be topping the bill at theatres and getting an awful lot more than I had been. Having left the band my personal life also started to pick up . . . after eight years of worshipping Henry, I now noticed other men.

I met an American performer called Carl Yale. He had a big music-publishing business in Denmark Street and I used to sing his songs. We started to go out with each other and I began to think that maybe we might have a future together. He was a kind and generous man, and it was easy to fall in love with him. Then one night Freda and I were taking a taxi through London and saw him with his arms round a sailor coming out of a gents' toilet! And he'd been pestering me to marry him! Well, that was that. We still remained friends because I loved him dearly.

One day I was playing in Cardiff and Carl phoned me at the theatre. He proposed over the phone, saying he wanted to get a special licence and marry me at the weekend. I refused – there was no way I was marrying a chap who enjoyed the company of sailors – so he threatened to marry another singer, Pat Taylor. I told him to go ahead. That Saturday I left Cardiff and went to Weston-Super-Mare to make a recording. He phoned me again and burst into tears. He said he'd married Pat but walked out on her after seeing her without her clothes on. He rushed down to me and was a complete wreck. I was very glad I hadn't agreed to marry him! Later he went to America where he married again and had twins. He came to England in 1976 for my night on *This Is Your Life* but just afterwards he slipped in the shower and died.

I was signed up as a regular in a new radio show featuring two comics, Jimmy Jewel and Ben Warriss. They were cousins who had worked together for years. In the sixties Jimmy became famous as Eli Pledge in the Granada TV comedy *Nearest and Dearest*. The pair were renowned for not getting on in real life, and I spent six weeks working in the most dreadful atmosphere. Jimmy wouldn't rehearse and Ben was a keen worker, so there was always conflict between the two. I'll never forget one rehearsal to which Jimmy actually turned up. The three of us stood in a row, me between the two men. We sang a song then had a comedy routine to get through, but they weren't on speaking terms and passed notes to each other through me. This went on for a while, but in the end I wouldn't play their silly game and told them to leave me out of their arguments. I would have left the show if I hadn't enjoyed my spot in it so much. It was a very popular little slot where I would take an old song, such as 'Just Like The Ivy' or 'Two Little Girls In Blue', and have it put to a super-modern rhythm. I used to get wonderful write-ups for that spot.

The Jewel and Warriss Show had a guest spot each week, which was normally filled with a male singer. One week, though, we had a young comic called Tony Hancock, and I've never seen anyone so nervous in my life. He was an absolute wreck and couldn't stop shaking. We had to talk him out of his dressing-room and on to the stage. I was amazed to see how different he was in front of the audience. He was a brilliant man but I thought he should have just given up on the business; it wasn't right to be so terrified of performing.

I spent the latter end of the 1940s working back in variety, no longer 'Betty Driver the Dynamic Juvenile' I was now 'Betty Driver, Star of Radio and Screen'. My film days were behind me, although I continued making radio broadcasts, with programmes such as *Fanfare*, which was recorded in Manchester, at the Apollo Ballroom, and *Northern Lights*, recorded in Southport. Despite my sophisticated singing act and the international acclaim I had received with Henry, it was always the warm north country welcome that I appreciated the most.

On 22 June 1949 the BBC aired a one-off radio broadcast, which lasted only fifteen minutes. It was called *Re-enter Betty Driver* and was a tester to see if the audiences who had loved me when I'd sung with Henry were interested enough in me to listen to my own show. I knew there was a lot riding on the success of the show and I was a bag of nerves standing in front of the microphone at eight-fifteen that night. I must have done something right, though, because the size of the postbag from listeners keen to hear more led the BBC to contact my agent with the offer of my own series. The first edition of *A Date With Betty* was broadcast live from the People's Palace in Poplar in the East End of London on 14 July, less than a month after the test broadcast. I was paid twenty-five guineas per show, of which there were sixteen half-hour broadcasts, going out between six forty-five and seven fifteen every Thursday evening.

The show's format was based around me singing, doing sketches and introducing guests. During the run of the series I took no other engagements and concentrated on organizing and rehearsing the shows. All my words were scripted by a young writer named Bob Monkhouse. He wrote fabulously for me. The BBC booked my guests and we tried out new acts as well as established stars. One of these acts was to change my life for ever.

The Peterson Brothers were South African, Wally and Mervyn, who played the guitar and sang. Their act was strong and modern. I fell for Wally in a big way. He was very good-looking, slim with a pencil moustache. He still had a deep tan, despite our colder climate, and was tall, with a great sense of humour. Freda met him before I did: she'd arrived at the theatre in Poplar and called into the hall-keeper's office for a key. Wally heard her addressed as Miss Driver and assumed that she was me. He was charming to her until he realized she was my sister, then turned the charm on me. And he had a great deal of charm. He didn't smoke or drink and he loved animals, and I soon found myself falling for him.

Unfortunately my series was not recommissioned: the producer, Glen Jones, complained that my mother, who turned up from time to time, made recordings a nightmare by dictating what material I used and how Bob wrote my scripts. He was quite right but I was too much in love to notice what was going on until it was too late. Once again my interfering mother had ruined a chance for me.

However, the BBC knew I was popular and kept giving me work in other shows. Throughout most of 1950 I appeared each week singing in a programme called *John Bull's Band* and when I wasn't working on that I could be found on *Star Spot, Music Hall, Worker's Playtime, Variety Band Box, Variety*

Fanfare, Curtain Up, Radio Parade and a host of shows on independent radio. I was touring left, right and centre, running up and down the country driving my Armstrong Siddeley and very happy . . . now that I was not so lonely: where possible my agent would get the Peterson Brothers put on the same bill as me.

My relationship with Wally picked up speed and early in 1951 we decided to live together. This was Wally's idea but I went happily along with it. Freda returned to Manchester but I was so involved with Wally and my new exciting life that I hardly noticed she had gone. He'd succeeded in alienating her from me without me noticing. I rented a bungalow in Finchley, which had once belonged to Gracie Fields' sister. Actually, I'd only just moved in when this woman in a headscarf called and said she was my next-door neighbour. That was Vera Lynn. We'd never really worked together in the past, although our paths had crossed, but we had so much in common and so many mutual friends that we met up for a chat every now and again.

Vera Lynn wasn't my only new acquaintance. The old world of variety was making way for the new fresh talents of stars who had learnt their craft in entertainment troupes during the war. The acts I had grown up with were leaving the business, through death or retirement, and young, dynamic, energetic performers were taking their place. In December 1951 I appeared as a guest on the radio show of a hilarious comic, Frankie Howerd, and I'm glad to say we hit it off immediately. In those days his act was classy and he was always well dressed. He had recently quit hosting *Variety Bandbox* and invited me to sing on his new show, *Fine Goings On* which was written by Eric Sykes and also starred Hattie

Jacques. Then Frankie asked me to go to Hamburg with him and we put on a show over there.

We did quite a lot of broadcasts in Hamburg for the troops there. One night he asked me to go out into the town with him. He took me to the red-light district and into a sleazy little club where all these beautiful topless girls were waitressing, just wearing tiny aprons. They were all over him, sitting on his lap. After a while I'd had enough and said I didn't think it was very nice. He told me not to be daft and I asked why he put up with the girls, knowing he was gay. He laughed and said they were all fellas! I was stunned. I'd had no idea!

Frankie and I shared a love of dogs, and he told me he wanted to buy a boxer. I told him that the next time he played Manchester he should visit Freda because she was breeding them. He went along and selected a dog but wouldn't stop pestering Freda after that, asking her out and saying he fancied her. She said, 'Hang on, I thought you were homosexual.' He said, 'Yes I am, but I've changed for you. There's only two women I've ever fancied – you and Joan Greenwood.' Poor Freda! What a compliment!

In 1952 the BBC gave me my very own television series, *The Betty Driver Show*, which they broadcast live from their studios at Lime Grove. I believe I was one of the first women to have her own entertainment series on television. The world of television was so different in those days: we only had one channel and technology was limited. Nothing was recorded and, of course, videotape didn't exist. We had to perform everything live to the camera and straight into people's living rooms! Everything was spontaneous and there were no autocues, so every line had to be learnt.

The Betty Driver Show was broadcast in cramped conditions from a tiny studio. We had two or three cameras, which were large and bulky, but their movement was restricted by the sea of cables that covered the studio floor, some of which were as large as the hoses used by the fire brigade. But in spite of this there was glamour. I wore spectacular evening gowns, and the band had to wear suits and bow-ties. My darling poodles ran about the set as I sat by the baby grand selecting songs to sing.

One of my guests on the show was my favourite funny man of the period, Tommy Cooper. That incredible dry, buffoon-like act of his! I would watch it through tears of mirth and admiration.

Early in 1952 Lew Grade put Tommy and me in a show together, along with the Peterson Brothers and my best friend in the business, the talented black pianist Winifred Atwell, 'the queen of honky-tonk'. We toured all over the country, playing at all of Lew's fabulous theatres. I soon realized just what a mop-head Tommy was, and it became my job to make sure that he arrived at the new theatre each Sunday without getting lost. I'd set off with Wally and my dogs in my estate car, filled with my trunk containing dresses, band parts, makeup and everything else I needed, and following on behind, in his tiny sports car, would be Tommy, along with his wife, who he called Dove. I'd drive with one eye on the road and the other on the rear-view mirror, making sure he was still with me. The first week we'd gone thirty miles when his car stopped. He said it had broken down but I realized he'd run out of petrol. He was so dozy that he hadn't even thought to fill the tank. From then on, every Saturday I'd make him fill up with petrol and I carried an extra can of petrol in my car just in case.

He was a sociable man who never wanted to go to sleep. Wally and I had to stop staying in the same hotel as the Coopers because he would keep us up all night chatting and testing out gags. But he was so funny and so kind-hearted. After working with him I always tried to catch his performances on television and I shall never forget watching him die on screen. The show was *Live From Her Majesty's* in 1984. When I saw him slide down the curtains I knew he was dead. Dove was backstage and she just pulled the curtain round him. It was a terribly sad moment.

I adored Lew Grade. I first met him when he and his brothers, Leslie Grade and Bernard Delfont, had a dancing act. Lew gave up the act and went into management and agency work. He was a wonderful boss to work for. I toured several variety shows with him in the late forties and he always treated his performers with style and respect. We felt we were stars on his circuits.

Winifred Atwell once threw a party in her house near St Albans for an American singer called Billy Eckstine. Wally and I went along and there was Bernard Delfont, dripping in gold jewellery. He had followed Lew into management, having given up the dance act he'd had with his partner, Kiki. His was one of the worst acts I'd ever seen. He was like an elephant, and just as cumbersome, while she was Oriental and small. He had only one step – a time step, repeated over and over. I'd lost count of the number of times we'd appeared on the same bill and I used to say to Lew, 'They're awful,' and he'd say, 'I know, but I like to give our Bernie a bit of work.' At this party I sneaked up to him and said, 'You were the worst act I've ever seen in my life!' Bernard agreed: 'Wasn't I bloody dreadful!'

Winifred, dear Winifred, played the piano as if her fingers were caressing the keys. She'd been born in Trinidad and had been a child prodigy before studying music in New York and London. We met first of all when we were booked on the same bill by Lew and we clicked immediately. Even when we weren't working together we'd meet up on Sundays to entertain servicemen who were still in hospital. She was a very generous woman but she was married to a complete brute. His name was Lew Levisohn and he was a retired comic turned theatrical agent and manager.

I remember playing with her once in Portsmouth. Winnie did fifteen minutes with a honky-tonk piano and a grand piano. It was a heavy act to do night after night and, to make matters worse, a boil came up under her arm. She showed it to me – a massive thing it was – and she was so upset because she was in agony and didn't know how she was going to play. I bathed it for her but she was still in pain. Her husband Lew wasn't at all sympathetic and said to me, 'Take no notice, these black 'uns cope with all sorts.'

Disgusted, I rounded on him: 'If I ever hear you refer to her like that again I'll thump you.' He was awful. He'd ignore her, smack her in the face and laugh at her. He was just after her money. That boil caused her so much pain that during one performance she fainted across the piano and had to be carried off.

Another new friend was the versatile Bruce Forsyth. Wally and I got to know him and his wife Penny very well. We never worked together but our paths would cross on the circuits. Val Parnell discovered him and put him on television in *Saturday Night at the Palladium*, making him a huge star. He was a fabulous all-rounder, a great dancer and

Living it up with Henry Hall and the boys – such sophistication!

Setting off for a six week ENSA tour of Europe, all dressed in Khaki with pips on my shoulder.

My wedding. Note Mother's happy expression.

My brief career as a blonde in the mid-fifties. My husband Wally was full of ideas on how I should alter my appearance.

Feeling uncomfortable in one of Wally's chosen dresses.

With my beloved Mitzi.

Dogs have always played a big part in my life. Here I am with Boxers Zoe and Polly, bred by Freda, and a little Cavalier named Lucy.

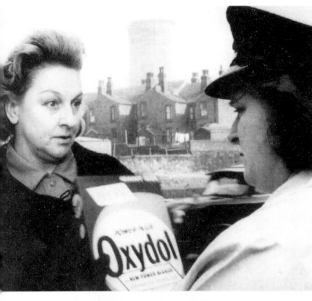

One of my appearances as Mrs Blunt, urging a Lollipop Lady to buy Oxydol, the only powder able to get her white coat glistening.

What A Racket with Arthur Askey, Blackpool 1961 – not the most enjoyable of theatrical runs.

A photograph to bring back horrible nightmares – rehearsing the judo throws with Arthur Lowe for my last appearance in *Pardon The Expression*.

William Moore played Cyril, Betty Turpin's policeman husband. This was our first publicity still together in 1969.

A *Street* scene with my screen son Gordon, played by Bill Kenwright. He never forgets me on Mothers' Day and always sends me beautiful flowers.

Being lifted by helicopter in 1981 after Freda had waved it down with a tea towel!

Another fine mess! Julie and I struggle to keep straight faces during the *Street* drag show.

Jean Alexander and me showing off our coat hangers. We spent hours making them and selling them for charity.

With two of my favourite people. Bill Tarmey (Jack Duckworth) demonstrates his mind power, upsetting Sarah Lancashire (Raquel Wolstenhulme) who fears for the fate of the penny tower.

Taking a tour of Hollands factory to inspect the making of my hotpots. Don't we look a picture!

FRIENDS OF WEATHERFIELD HOSPITAL

pianist, but Val only saw him as a comedian and refused to let him do anything but compère and tell jokes.

Bruce was present at Burnt Oak Register Office when I married Wally on 19 December 1953. I hadn't really wanted to marry: I was happy enough living in Finchley with Wally and my dogs, Mitzi, Tina and Jackie, but Wally wanted marriage and was so insistent that I agreed. His brother Mervyn was best man, and a music publisher called Kay O'Dwyer, who was a great friend, was my attendant. Tommy Cooper came, as did my agents, the Azas, and my parents. The only person who didn't attend was Freda. Mother insisted she remained in Manchester and, actually, I think that if she had turned up she would have tried to stop the ceremony somehow. She always felt that Wally was only interested in my bank account.

We had only one photograph taken and that made us look as though we were at a funeral. I was very slender then and wore a grey suit, a little hat and I carried a spray of orchids. I remember it all too clearly because I paid for the wedding, the reception and the ring. We had our reception at the Leicester Square Hotel but no honeymoon, and just carried on working as we had been booked to tour in all Val Parnell's theatres around the country.

Before the wedding, Wally had started to change the way I looked and sang. Up to this point I'd always worn glamorous gowns for my act, graceful, sophisticated outfits that fell to the floor. I'd pin flowers to my chest and had my hair piled on top of my head. Wally said that look was too dated. He wanted me in short knee-length wide skirts, which I loathed, with satin tops and bows. Very Alma Cogan. I liked all my dresses to be different but he ordered six in exactly the same style, just different colours. It drove me mad but I went along with it because I loved him.

Then he started on my style. I was known for singing a certain style of song and had always gone down well wherever I'd performed. I was a vivacious singer and that's what the public expected of me. Now Wally decided he wanted me to sing like Peggy Lee, or Lena Horne, saying my act was corny. He played me loads of Peggy's records and told me to start phrasing like her but I said it didn't suit me. When I tried but it didn't work he called me old-fashioned and got at me, wearing me down. Eventually I became very cowed and did as he said, as I had with Mother. We toured with this new look and new singing style and suddenly audiences were lukewarm: they knew I couldn't do the new songs. The audience proved my point, but Wally wouldn't have any of it. For the first time since joining Henry Hall I began to dread going on-stage.

One day Val Parnell phoned and asked me to deputize for Joy Nichols at the London Hippodrome that evening. Luckily I'd shampooed the dogs! Joy was a famous radio comedian in *Take It From Here*, which starred Jimmy Edwards and was written by Frank Muir and Dennis Norden. The show was Joy's but Val said all I'd have to do was my normal act, with Wally, my pianist and the dogs. We had no time to rehearse but, thankfully, everything went well and the audience was happy. Joy was ill so Val asked me to stay for the week but after that I went on to the next theatre where I was booked.

A fortnight later he was back on the phone begging me to return to the Hippodrome because Joy was ill again. This happened about four times and I complained to Val that my tour was being disrupted. He told me not to worry as he could find cover for me but I refused to do it any more – I didn't like deputizing for Joy all the time. I carried on with my tour, and Joy's show finished in London then went to Australia. Two days after she'd flown out I had another call from Val: Joy was ill, would I take over the show? He told me to ignore the fact that I had a sixteen-week tour planned and said I had three days to pack before flying out to Australia with Wally. I wasn't allowed to take the dogs or my pianist.

My pianist was a wonderful man named Alan Kitson. Every Monday morning, wherever we were playing, he'd have a little bunch of flowers put in my dressing room. He always gave me confidence because he knew how I breathed and how I phrased. When you start to rehearse with a new pianist it's like going to the doctor for the first time: you don't know what to do or what to tell them. I used to work to the audience: if they were good I'd have a joke with them, or if not I'd carry straight through with the act, and Alan knew exactly what I was doing the whole time.

He was a fine pianist, and I tried to insist that he came with me, but Val assured me I wouldn't need him as there were excellent pianists in Australia. So, there we were, Wally and I, flying half-way round the world to stand in for an ill singer.

I landed in Sydney and was met by the manager of the theatre, who astounded me with his first words, 'Isn't it a cow of a day?' I'd never been around people who spoke like that, and I hadn't been prepared for it. He dumped us at the hotel and we went into the restaurant for some breakfast. When I ordered toast and marmalade the waitress had a laughing fit and said they only served eight- or sixteen-ounce steaks with eggs on and asked how many eggs I wanted. Straight away I was marked out as a strange Englishwoman.

I was worried about performing without Alan so I took all my music with me to the theatre and asked to meet the pianist. It turned out that he was the pit pianist and had no experience of playing in an act. We had three days to rehearse, with me explaining how I sang each song, but he couldn't memorize the tunes and had to work with the sheets of music at the side of the piano, in full view of the audience.

On opening night I died a death – like a lead balloon. No response. Nothing. And there I was with a six-month booking ahead of me. The manager asked if I had some older songs because no one knew the ones I was singing. I searched around and came up with old numbers which I hated. I could put up with that, though, because it made sense to give the audience songs they knew. However, the manager had another demand to make: that I remove Wally from the act. I couldn't understand why but the manager insisted that he was moved off the stage. Apparently Joy Nichols' husband was called Wally Petersen and the audience would think I'd muscled in on her show and stolen her husband. My husband was Peter*son* and not Peter*sen*, but that made no difference. I ended up doing a thirty-minute act with a naff pianist, no husband, no dogs, and for the first fortnight I died the death of a duck, just like the first night, until I worked out what they wanted to hear.

The rest of the performers and the stage crew refused to speak to me unless I asked them a direct question. That was because I was English and they thought me stuck up, mainly because I objected to their foul language.

The microphone rose up from beneath the stage and every night they'd put it in the wrong position, either too high or too low, and I'd have to compensate by changing the volume of my singing. After a fortnight I'd had enough. I came off the stage and called everyone together, 'If any of you bastards dare do any more to cripple my act I'll close the show!' At that they all smiled, and said at last I was one of them. That was all it took – a swear word!

The same night they set up a party on the stage with barrels of beer, food and wine, and from then on I was a riot in Australia. I did broadcasts and interviews and was always well received.

Accepting the swearing wasn't the only adjustment I was forced to make. Every Friday in England the theatre manager would pay the artists for the week's work, starting with the number-one dressing room and working down. That was his main job, to pay the artists. In Australia I was told I had to line up outside the manager's office where he would pay me along with everyone else – the other acts, the chorus, the stage-hands and cleaners. I was horrified and asked the manager to pay me in my dressing-room: I was the star, it was my show, and I didn't want everyone else knowing how much I was paid. He refused and insisted I queued with the others but I wasn't having that. From then on I sent Wally up to sign for my money.

I found out where Joy was in hospital and decided to go to see her. I didn't know what was wrong with her but then discovered she was suffering psychiatric problems. Wally and I found her sitting on her bed. I introduced myself to her and she stared at me and demanded, 'How long have you been sleeping with my husband?' I said, 'I haven't,' but she was adamant. 'Oh, yes, you have. Wally Petersen.' I tried to explain that my Wally was South African and hers was Canadian, but she was having none of it. Then she said, 'You took over from me at the London Hippodrome, didn't you? Well, the next time you're there go into the dressing-room and clear up all that dog shit you left all over the carpet.' I was shocked to the core: my dogs were very clean and I certainly had *not* let them do that. The poor woman was deranged.

Every Wednesday we played a matinée, and after a while I began to notice that the same two people occupied the same front-stall seats each week. They always cheered and clapped louder than anyone else. Then, before the performance, I started to receive from them a beautiful corsage of stephanotis, waxen white flowers that smelt beautiful. After six weeks I invited them backstage to my dressing-room. From my view on the stage they'd always looked a bit wild, like hillbillies, but when I saw them up close I was staggered. The woman had on a Stetson, with what looked like a piece of costume jewellery six inches long pinned to one side of it, and a filthy brown coat with a fur round her neck that was so old it looked like a dead rat. Across her chest she had another great lump of jewellery. Her hands were covered in rings, yet her nails were filthy. I said it was lovely to see them and thanked them for the flowers. The woman said, 'Why don't you come over and see us?' It turned out they lived six hundred miles away and flew in each week in their own plane, just to see my show. I hadn't time to visit them but they became regular visitors backstage. I discovered that they were sheep farmers, that the jewellery was all real and that they were billionaires. It just goes to show that you shouldn't judge a book by its cover!

After Sydney I took the show to Melbourne. I liked Australia but it was so hot, and everyone drank so much. You'd see men carrying grog bags around with them, black bags like the sort doctors carried. Apparently the licensing laws forced all the pubs to close at six o'clock at night so the men drank all day and during the last hour had their bags filled with drink. They would take them to the park, and sit opposite the theatre stage door, then drink until they passed out. Later the police would arrive and throw them into a wagon. I found it all rather seedy and squalid.

When my six months was up, I was glad to return to England. I'd been long enough in the company of my husband to realize that marrying him had been a dreadful mistake. He made no attempt to hide his roving eye. We would be walking down a street together and if he saw a girl he liked he'd stop her and say, 'You are so beautiful,' with me right next to him, feeling ugly and humiliated. Still, I told myself, it was because we were abroad and once we returned to England everything would get back to normal.

I was wrong.

CHAPTER TWELVE

My South African Nightmare

The trip to Australia had left me exhausted and I was hoping for some time off, perhaps to take a much-needed holiday, but this was not to be as my agent had been busy in my absence, booking engagements at theatres across the country. I'm not a person who keeps many cuttings or reviews but one that I do have dates back to this time in 1953, from one of my first performances after Australia, at the Palace Theatre in Blackpool:

> In the variety world they say that Betty Driver is the most appropriately named artist in the business. She is one of the most forceful performers on the boards. How true. Her reappearance in town was accorded an impressive ovation. Miss Driver gave us 100 per cent of her best and demonstrated once again what an important thing personality is.

I won't bother with any more reviews in case I get accused of being big-headed, but that writer was right about one thing: I always gave 100 per cent. I was an old-timer, from the days of the variety greats and one lesson I'd learnt early on was that the audience had paid hard-earned money to see me and they deserved the best I could give them – bang, straight between the eyes. That was one area where my husband and I disagreed: he thought you could cut corners. I knew different.

Giving 100 per cent was difficult in 1953 as I suffered great discomfort with my periods. I had discovered I was pregnant but sadly miscarried. Wally wanted children and I was eager to please him but it wasn't to be. The doctors discovered I had fibroids in the womb and insisted on a hysterectomy. Of course, being a trouper, I'd always carried on working during my periods but the pain became almost more than I could bear until, one day in Dudley, I haemorrhaged. I was doubled over in agony but Wally insisted I went on and did the show or we wouldn't be paid. I went on, smiling and singing all these daft chirpy numbers, and the next day I was in hospital, having the operation.

When I came home I was greeted by a caring Wally, who told me, 'There's the chicken. There are the potatoes. Put the dinner on. I'm off to play golf.' Within two weeks I was working again. I didn't object. After all, I'd been brought up to follow orders. It was heart-wrenching to know I'd never have a child, so shortly afterwards we looked into adoption, but were turned down because I was constantly on the move. It wouldn't have been fair on a child to leave it all the time, but I would have loved a little boy or girl of my own.

So, I was soon back to work and although the routine

remained the same – driving around the country from theatre to theatre, digs to digs – and the theatres beckoned me, the faces of my fellow performers were continuing to change. One of the biggest names in showbusiness at the time was an organist named Reginald Dixon. He had his own radio show, which was broadcast from the Tower Ballroom, Blackpool, where he was the resident organist. I did a couple of the shows with him, a disastrous experience: when you sing with an organ there's a time lapse between you and it, with the organ two or three beats behind. Reginald played full pelt as it was his show and drowned me completely.

Around this time I appeared in a huge revue for charity, *An American Comic and Seventy Women*. It was based around the simple idea of Jackie Mason, the comic, telling gags and introducing seventy of us, all star artists. I couldn't name them all but I know Anne Shelton, Vera Lynn, Florence Desmond, Kitty Bluett, Evelyn Laye and Sabrina were there. Twelve of us had to share one dressing room, and I'll never forget our fury when we learnt that Gracie Fields had one to herself, with champagne and flowers . . . *and* she got paid. A charity revue and she was paid! The rest of us weren't given so much as a cup of tea.

Sabrina was a sweet girl who didn't do much. At one time she worked with Arthur Askey, just walking on and off the stage, looking stunning. She was a gimmick: tall with a huge bust. Her real name was Norma Sykes and we liked each other straight away, but nobody else would talk to her. Whilst we rehearsed the revue she sat in the corner and looked worried. I asked her what the matter was and she told me she'd forgotten to bring her corset and couldn't go on without it. I sent a taxi to her house to collect it and I couldn't believe my eyes when it arrived: it was a huge contraption with metal supports to push up her bosom. I helped her put it on. Naked she looked terribly misshapen: tiny waist and gigantic chest. Renee Houston looked her up and down and said, 'Well, it's the first time I've seen tits top of the bill!'

As I've said, it was always important for me to give of my best. It was drilled into me so hard so young that the habit has never left me, but I've been amazed at some performers' attitude towards their work. I'll never forget a show I did for Moss Empires, in Glasgow. I was top of the bill and the booking agent asked if I minded an extra act being put in the show as they wanted to give this young man a chance. Now, Glasgow Empire was a comedian's graveyard; no English comic ever got a titter there. So this young man, a new singer and comic, arrived with his band parts but they were all songs I was singing in the show so I found him others. He was entirely unprepared. He knocked on my dressing-room door for soap and makeup and had nothing to wear so my husband lent him a suit. I was furious: it was a number-one date and he had put no effort into it. He went on stage and I watched from the side. He did a monologue called 'Six Feet Under'. The audience ate him alive! He was booed off the stage! He had no idea about timing or delivery and his act went on and on for about fifteen minutes. It was like watching someone die on that stage. If I hadn't been so annoyed by his unprofessional approach I'd have felt sorry for him, but I couldn't help thinking he'd brought it on himself.

Although the war was over there were still plenty of

troops overseas in administration or sorting out conflicts, and they needed entertaining. I was asked by ENSA to get together a troupe and we were sent to Malta. The troupe consisted of myself, Wally, the Darby Quintette, a beautiful soubrette and a ventriloquist. It was winter and we toured all the Army camps, putting up our staging and belting out numbers, encouraging the lads to sing along. It was my first time in Malta and I had no idea how prudish the locals were. One day, in Valetta, the sun came out so I took everyone down to the beach to sunbathe. I was wearing trousers and a black top but I didn't want marks on my skin because of the dresses I wore in my act, so I left my neck and shoulders exposed, with no straps holding my top up. We all sat on the beach, beneath a wall. All of a sudden some coins were thrown over the wall at me, which I thought very odd. Then two Maltese policemen turned up, grabbed me under my arms and frogmarched me off the beach. I tried to protest but they had me in a strong grip and were shouting at me. They demanded to know where I was staying and, thankfully, the hotel manager spoke good English. It transpired that they had thought I was a prostitute because I was wearing a strapless top and the coins had been thrown by hopeful chaps! The hotel manager said it wouldn't have mattered how little I wore in the summer but things were different in winter. To them I was immoral and indecent. And the only part of me on view had been my shoulders!

During the war in 1956, I took the same show to Cyprus, for the Foreign Office. Some Cypriot guerrillas were in revolt against British rule and a bloody conflict ensued. We were stationed in Famagusta, Kyrenia and Nicosia, entertaining troops who had been sent out to protect Britain's interests. It was very dangerous and we were only allowed out if we were guarded. There were snipers everywhere. One day the CO said we'd have to get up early the next morning as we had to go to the top of a mountain because the Red Berets' garrison was there. The next day we got into the Army lorry, about six men, me and another girl. The local boy who was meant to drive the lorry kept having fainting fits so he wasn't allowed to drive us that day, and no one was available to take over. We realized that one of us would have to do it. All the men refused because the road was narrow and it was a sheer drop to one side so, nothing else for it, I had to drive. Boulders fell around us as I manoeuvred that great lorry along the tiny track. It was very hairy at times, and my husband looked as if he was going to be sick all the way, but I was so proud of myself when I got us safely to the top.

The same trip found us stopping at a little café to use the toilet. Whilst we were there I saw a jar of pickled onions on the bar. I love pickled onions so I asked for one. Then I had a closer look at the jar. What I had taken for onions were tiny pickled birds. Apparently the locals trapped them by nailing pieces of wood to the walls then painting them with a strong glue so that when the birds came to rest they couldn't escape. They died and were pickled. I carried on so much about it, shouting at the café proprietor that it was the most disgusting thing I'd ever seen in my life, that Wally had to drag me out, fearing I'd be arrested – again!

Almost as soon as we got home from Cyprus I was asked to take another troupe out to the Middle East, to Jordan and Egypt where, again, there was rebellion against British rule. It was even more dangerous there, and we had an armed guard everywhere we went. When we drove from place to place in the lorry there would be a soldier up front with a gun and one at the back, always on the lookout. We finished a show in Amman and were about to leave when the hotel owner arrived and boarded up the windows. We were forced to stay inside and all around us we could hear gunfire. We were worried because we had to catch a plane to our next show in Ismailiyah, so we were smuggled out of the back way and driven to the airport. We were thrown aboard the plane and took off in a rush, just as a bomb was fired at us. It exploded below us and thankfully the tail end was only slightly damaged.

We had to fly five hundred miles across Egypt to give a show at eight o'clock in the morning – any later and the sun would have been too hot to be outside. The troops had rigged up a stage on the beach, covered with sheets to give me some shade and the lads all lay in the sea to keep cool.

One night, the CO drove us into the desert in jeeps. It was very eerie. We arrived at a little oasis where they'd prepared an arena and surrounded it with chairs, sofas and lamps. The officers were sitting around being served by local men all dressed in white. It was just like a film set. They asked me not to start singing until a sheikh appeared so I sat and had a drink. All of a sudden search-lights from our oasis turned into the desert, and galloping towards us were several camels ridden by a troop of men all dressed in white flowing robes with fantastic scarlet turbans on their heads. Right at the front rode the sheikh. You could see him coming for miles because he was covered in diamonds from head to foot. It was a marvellous scene, with the dust from the camels' hoofs flying around them like a cloud, just like a sequence from *The Desert Song*. When they arrived I was introduced to the sheikh and admired a huge diamond ring he was wearing. He let me try it on and it weighed a ton. Then I sang for him until about three or four in the morning.

The following day the CO took me to the sheikh's palace, a sensational gold building set in the sand. He took me inside and I was amazed to find that the only furniture consisted of orange boxes. I was introduced to the sheikh's number-one wife: she was the most beautiful creature I'd ever seen. She was dripping with gold and jewels – they must have been worth enough to buy Buckingham Palace. She was wearing emerald green, pure silk tapered trousers, a bejewelled top, and her neck and arms were almost obscured by gold and rubies. She was stunning, completely stunning.

It was a far cry from the palace but I loved my new detached house in St Albans and was busy making it into a comfortable home. Wally, though, was growing bored with being part of my act and decided he wanted to become an agent. My friend Winifred Attwell's husband Lew was an agent so I bought Wally a partnership in Lew's business. They shared an office in Bond Street and he seemed happy enough. He looked after a few acts but I guessed it was only going to be a hobby for him. His real passion was golf: he was a talented player and could easily have turned professional. He had joined the Variety Artists Golfing Society and became their champion player. I started playing myself too but gave it up after he demanded to see what I'd learnt. I was so nervous of him that I couldn't hit the ball, and he heaped scorn on me. I flung my golf club at him and stormed off the course.

At St Albans I still had my beloved poodles and also a budgie. I was once at a garden centre with my cousin Joyce, the only cousin Freda and I have ever had anything to do with. We had the three poodles with us and were wandering around admiring a row of beautiful yellow chrysanthemums. I spotted a bird amongst the plants and handed the dogs to Joyce so that I could investigate. I crawled into the flower-bed and picked up this big, beautiful budgie, which looked as if a cat had had him. I held him in my hands and told the man at the garden-centre shop that I'd found him and left my address in case anyone reported a missing budgie.

On the way home Joyce sat in the back of the car with the dogs whilst I drove with the budgie clinging to my neck. I stopped off for bird seed and when I got home I found an old box and some chicken wire and made a cage, sticking a knitting needle into it for the budgie to perch on. He was absolutely worn out and just sat on the perch. He looked so miserable that I sat up all night with him, worrying. The next day my aunt bought me a cage on a stand and I put it in front of the window in the sunshine. He'd sit on his little swing but wouldn't speak.

One night my husband and I invited my pianist, Reg, and his mother to the house for dinner. The mother was very strict, very Methodist, little lace gloves and cherries in her hat. We sat in the dining-room and just as I was serving dinner there came this voice from the lounge, loud and all too clear: 'You bastard . . . yes, you bastard . . . Charlie's a good boy but you – you bastard!' The old lady put down her knife and fork and said, 'Reginald! Come on, we're going home!' and off they went. Once that bird had started he wouldn't stop. His language was dreadful. He swung on his little swing and swore all the time.

I had to go on tour so I left Charlie with Freda. When I got back she'd turned him into a right little goody-goody. She had discovered he liked to sit outside the cage and fly around the room and she'd tell him that if he didn't stop swearing she'd put him in the cage. And he was so naughty! If Dad was eating, Charlie would jump down on to the table and dive into his dinner! He'd go around the house sitting on Freda's head, fast asleep, and then he discovered the dogs and they all fell in love with him, about twelve of them, and let him sit on their heads. He was a fabulous bird and we were heartbroken when he died. When the vet looked at him he said he must have been over twenty, which is almost unheard-of in budgies. Even today I still miss him.

Mother died in 1956. She'd had a long illness and in the end it was lung cancer that claimed her. Freda was a star during the last few weeks of Mother's life. She knew I was busy working so didn't let me know she was any worse than usual. For three solid weeks she nursed Mother single-handed as Dad stayed out of the way. The last words Mother said to Freda were 'Forgive me.' Of course she did, and so I would have done too: yes, she'd been a hard woman but she was still my mother. When Freda phoned with the news of her death I fainted. It seems strange to think now how she dominated my childhood, how she pushed me into show business then struggled to keep me at the top. She'd taken so much from me: my childhood, my self-esteem, my money, my happiness, but even so I mourned her. She had cardiac asthma and had neglected her health terribly, carting me around the country. When she died Freda was in a terrible state: not only had she nursed her twenty-four hours a day but Dad had retired from the police force and just sat about the house all day. The thought of looking after him for the rest of his life nearly drove her to suicide.

To make matters worse they were living in a huge, rambling twenty-one-roomed house called Moorfield in Kersal that I had bought originally in 1946 when Dad retired. My parents had said they wanted to run a country club so the house was bought for this purpose. I furnished it and Dad got a licence and opened a classy establishment. Poor Freda did all the work; Mother sat and talked to the customers and Dad counted the money. Freda served, cooked and cleaned, and wasn't even paid a wage.

Then Dad took up serving after hours. Of course he was caught and charged. The magistrate was prepared to let him off with a warning but Freda refused to run the club unless she was paid. Dad said there was no way he was paying his own daughter so the club closed and the house became their home. Then Freda started to breed dogs, poodles and boxers, and kept them in kennels there.

In 1957 I made an appearance on BBC television's *The Good Old Days* at Leeds City Varieties. It was wonderful and I was paid the princely sum of fifty guineas. I was done up as Florrie Ford, the big music-hall star, in a sensational outfit, fitted in London, a gorgeous black velvet gown with long sleeves and a huge hat with feathers in. I used a long cane with a diamond handle, just like Florrie's, and sang 'It's A Long Way To Tipperary'. Oh, I did enjoy that.

Of course, it goes without saying that whilst my professional life was busy and fulfilling, my personal life was in tatters. Wally would go off each day to play golf or at being an agent and one night he came home with a black eye. He wouldn't tell me how he got it so I asked Lew, who said he'd thumped Wally after finding him straddled over the desk with a chorus girl. He said it had been going on for months, a different girl every day. Lew had finally had enough and hit him, on my behalf.

I couldn't leave him. I didn't have the nerve. His brow-beating had destroyed my self-confidence just as my mother's had. Just like her, he now dictated everything I did. But I'd already guessed he'd been seeing other women and now I knew for sure. That didn't stop him. He carried on sleeping around and I put up with it, thinking that marriage was for life, good or bad.

One day Wally woke me up and said, 'I'm going home.' I told him not to be so daft, that he was home already. But he didn't mean home in St Albans, he meant home in South Africa. He said he'd had enough of England, that it was a pig-hole and that I had to pack up the house and follow him. Of course I wasn't happy with that idea: I loved England, I had my family, my home, my career, but of course he didn't have anything like that. He only had me, and I wasn't enough for him. However, I convinced myself that it was my duty to be with him, and two months after he'd gone he instructed me to sell the house, the car and my jewellery, to put the dogs down and catch a boat to

South Africa. Like a fool I did everything he said, apart from killing the dogs: I sent them to live with Freda in Manchester. The voyage took me two weeks and when we docked in Cape Town, Wally met me and said, 'You look a damned mess.' No big hello, no kisses, no flowers.

Wally had used money I'd sent over to buy himself a theatrical agency in Johannesburg. He had a big suite of offices but had given hardly any thought to a home. He had rented this grubby little flat in a tower block and dumped me there. It had lino floors, twin beds, and was very shabby. I'd managed to bring some of my furniture and ornaments over on the boat but they didn't make much difference. He went to the office every day but refused to let me anywhere near it, and I was trapped in the flat. His mother lived nearby and I went to visit her. She scowled at me and demanded to know when I was going to start having children. I explained that I couldn't because of my operation. She laughed and said that without children I'd never keep Wally. Indeed, I hardly ever saw him. It was the same old story: he'd be having fun with chorus girls in his office then stay out until the early hours of the morning spending my money.

When it was discovered that I was in South Africa I started to get offers of work, singing in high-class clubs, but whenever I went to talk to producers about a show they all said they wouldn't have Wally as part of my act. That was fine by me but Wally wouldn't have it: if I was going to be in a big show he wanted to be included. This happened time and time again and I was turning down over a thousand pounds a week, before I discovered that no club or theatre would employ a Peterson. I don't know why, they just wouldn't. I was in South Africa for four months and never worked.

One morning, at about four o'clock, Wally woke me up when he came in and told me he was in love with a girl he'd seen in an audience but to whom he had never spoken. I said, 'Are you sure?' and when he said he was, I decided I'd had enough. The next morning I startled him by turning up at his office and asked his secretary to put a call through to Freda in England. It took about two hours to set it up and when I heard her voice I just broke down and said, 'I want to come home, I'm so unhappy.' Freda said, 'Come home, then,' but I said I couldn't because Wally had spent all my money. Thankfully I'd left money in my bank in England so Freda arranged for some to be transferred to South Africa and gave strict instructions that it was only to be given to me and no one else.

A few days later I set off to the bank, but Wally insisted on coming with me. When we arrived the manager gave me an air ticket to England and two hundred pounds. Wally asked what was going on, so the manager told him I was leaving. Wally demanded half of the money and said I was welcome to go because I was of no use to him. The bank manager refused to let him have it, saying it was mine and mine alone.

As soon as we got outside Wally shouted at me and called me all sorts of names. I broke down and ended up giving him almost all of the money. He allowed me to keep seven pounds. I had to leave all my furniture and what was left of my clothes and caught the plane back to London then flew on to Manchester. By the time I arrived at Freda's I didn't even have enough money to pay off the taxi. He took everything I had, everything. I was completely broken. We'd been married for seven years and 1960 found me alone, back in England.

CHAPTER THIRTEEN

The Television Personality

My return to England was far from glorious. I brought with me just two suitcases and an empty purse. As well as my beautiful clothes and jewels, I had also left my self-esteem in South Africa. Mother was dead, and Freda and Dad were living in the country house I'd helped Dad buy in Kersal. I dumped myself on them and for twelve months couldn't face returning to the theatre. I sat about moping until Freda decided to occupy me in her poodle parlour. As well as breeding show dogs, Freda also groomed other people's dogs and I used to shampoo them and make little coats to sell to women with more money than sense.

I was content doing this but Freda and my agent refused to let me vegetate. They talked me into taking a booking in Blackpool for a comedy stage play. The sad thing was that by this time, after years of singing in smoky theatres, my voice was nearly gone. Over the years it had become lower and lower and now, just when I needed it to earn money, I couldn't sing. I'd overworked it and had had laryngitis for many years, but a stage play was something I thought I could manage. It was a new venture for me and I felt I could do justice to it. After all, I had good comic timing – I'd worked with enough comedians to learn that!

The play was a farce called *Pillar to Post*. I starred along-side Glenn Melvyn and Danny Ross, and the plot revolved around them playing two rival postmen. My character was married to Glenn's. It ran for twenty-two weeks at Blackpool's Grand Theatre and was a riot. It was the autumn of 1960 and I was unaware that just forty miles inland auditions were being held for a new twice-weekly family drama called *Florizel Street*. Actors from all over the north were being called up but I wasn't one of them: I was a singer who acted occasionally and, besides, I would be engaged in Blackpool throughout the six-week run of this new television show.

At the time, there was a Blackpool radio series called *Blackpool Nights*, which starred Jimmy Clitheroe, a popular northern comic, and a host of actors and actresses in semi-regular roles. One was a woman called Patricia Phoenix. She was a beautiful girl and I first met her backstage at the Grand. I didn't know who she was and had no idea that we'd first met as children, and had gone to the same school. I came off-stage at the Grand and there she was, watching the show from the wings. The first words she said to me were 'Could you lend me ten bob?' so I did. The next week she came for more money and it kept going up and up. After four times I refused and challenged her: I knew she was working. She told me that she'd had an audition for *Florizel Street* at Granada and it was for thirteen episodes. If she got the job she'd pay me back.

Of course she had a successful audition and was cast as

the world-weary siren, Elsie Tanner. *Florizel Street* never made it to the screens: the Granada tea lady was heard to comment that the title sounded like a brand of disinfectant. It was renamed and *Coronation Street* was born. Nine years later, when I joined the cast as Betty Turpin, Pat didn't remember to pay me back the money she owed me. She was a glamorous tryer, but she never did anyone any harm. Her tragedy was that she was surrounded by people who were jealous of her and made her life a misery. Women saw her as a rival, and men just took advantage of her.

I must have gone down well in Blackpool because the following year I was booked at the same theatre to appear in the summer-season show with Arthur Askey. It was called *What A Racket*, and Arthur and I took the parts of middle-aged parents living with their rock-and-roller of a son. It was a dreadful experience and I quickly learnt to loathe Arthur Askey. Our paths had never crossed in variety and I'd heard some say he was a selfish performer, but I tried to keep an open mind until I'd worked with people myself. At every entrance he made, he'd walk down to the footlights and say his catchphrase, 'I thank you.' In the middle of a play! Twenty-two weeks, eight shows a week! I felt like strangling him. When we opened the show the second half was a bit dreary so he suggested putting in a musical number. He was a pianist and suggested that he played whilst I sang. I refused, but he persisted and talked me into it. The number didn't stay in for long because he couldn't bear the applause I got.

I couldn't wait to leave that summer season but was wary of my next venture – another first. My agent, unable to book me variety any more, had become adventurous and had landed me a contract with Proctor and Gamble to star in a series of commercials for their soap products. I played a lady called Mrs Blunt and showed off my wonderful whites to the whole nation. We made five of these commercials a year in a studio in Brighton. We made them in batches – three one time, two six months later. I can't remember exactly how many I appeared in but I did my first in 1961 and the last in 1964, so there were a good few and as soon as they started going out I was grabbed in the street and asked about my whites.

Granada Television beckoned for the first time in 1962. I'd been aware of the company's presence in Manchester since 1956 and had been curious to see its new office block, it being the first custom-built television studio in Europe. Granada had the franchise to broadcast across the whole of the north of England, although in 1968 they lost the Yorkshire region. It was a powerful organization in a relatively new business, the Independent Television Network having only started up in 1955. It was my first television outside the BBC, whose offers of work had more or less dried up because I could no longer sing very well.

Granada booked me to take a role in a production of *Love on the Dole*, playing Mrs Blood, the local woman who brought on miscarriages. Anne Stallybrass and James Bolam were the two young stars and I had a great time in my role. I even had real leeches to bleed people with. I had a wonderful write-up in *The Times*: 'Betty Driver's brilliant cameo performance nearly stole the whole play. If she'd been in it more she would have done.'

This play was the only work I took outside my commercial contract during my three years as Mrs Blunt. That contract was strict and, I discovered, after attending an audition at Granada, very restricting. The last time I had auditioned for anything had been when I was fourteen, performing in front of the manager at the Prince of Wales theatre in London. Everything else had just been given to me but this role was different: it was the part of an interfering woman who was going to move into Coronation Street with her layabout husband. The *Street* had been running now for over three years, well exceeding its initial thirteen episodes. The cast had become household names and the writing was of the very best. It was a quality programme and I was keen to be part of it.

I sat in an office facing producer Harry Kershaw, casting director Jose Scott and writers Harry Driver and Vince Powell, and read for the part of Hilda Ogden. There was a great deal of whispering during my reading and confused expressions. They liked what I did but said that really they were looking for a little whippet of a woman but they wanted me so much, they said it didn't matter what I looked like. They offered me the role and Jose went off to contact my agent, who in turn contacted Proctor and Gamble. Of course, they wouldn't release me from my contract so that was the end of me playing Hilda Ogden. Freda was pleased because she hadn't liked the idea of me playing in curlers all the time – and I'm delighted that Jean Alexander was taken on in the role because she became one of my greatest friends. Ironically, six weeks after my audition Proctor and Gamble ended my contract.

I bowed out of radio in March 1965, not singing and laughing through sketches but acting in the J. B. Priestley play *When We Are Married*. It was for the BBC and was put out uninterrupted. It's a funny play concerning three middle-aged couples who discover, through no fault of their own, that they are not legally married. I played one of the wives, married to Frank Pettingell, and Thora Hird was another. We had to deliver our lines standing around a shared microphone, and Thora was the funniest woman ever. A wonderful comedienne, she had me in stitches throughout the whole recording. It was a hilarious show but such a struggle to record because every time I looked up from my script, she was pulling awful faces. I only had to look at her and I'd be laughing.

I was back at Granada in the summer of 1965, having been signed up for a new comedy series called *Pardon the Expression*, which was a spin-off from *Coronation Street*, following the fortunes of a popular character, Leonard Swindley, played by Arthur Lowe. In the *Street* he had left to take a job in the head office of the Gamma Garments stores. In this new show, Swindley had been made assistant manager of a department store called Dobson and Hawks. It was farce set amongst shop counters with middle-aged bosses and young shop girls, a forerunner of *Are You Being Served?* My character was a bossy Lancashire woman who ran the staff canteen and had a soft spot for Swindley. I enjoyed the experience no end. Each episode was recorded in front of a live audience so I was in my element, playing to them. In all we made thirty-two episodes over three years. Each season we seemed to become more and more over-the-top and unreal, but that's comedy, I suppose. Subtlety went out of the window.

Robert Dorning and Joy Stewart also starred in the series but we all knew it was just a vehicle for Arthur Lowe: he was a popular actor and Granada were desperate to hang on to him. I thought he was clever but I didn't enjoy working with him because he was a selfish actor. If, in reading through a script, one of my lines got a laugh it was cut and given to him. I remember one show in which he took every single one of my lines and I told the director I might as well go home because I had nothing left to say. Arthur didn't enjoy the recordings because he didn't welcome the audience and used to complain about them being there. I felt the opposite: I came alive in front of an audience. Most television actors hate audiences: their craft is to do with small gestures, inclines in the voice and delicate mannerisms. I can do all that but I just love hearing the rustle of sweet wrappers and laughs when I'm working.

Whilst making the series I became friendly with Eileen Derbyshire. She played spinster Emily Nugent in *Coronation Street* and was about to be written out of the series: she was pregnant in real life and was growing radiantly in size. Every week I'd catch up with her in the canteen and she'd tell me how her pregnancy was going. I was familiar with her acting as I watched the *Street* occasionally, thought it realistic and loved the characters. It was refreshing to see ordinary northern people portrayed in a real setting, loving and hurting, crying and laughing. I'd never lived in a terrace but I knew plenty of people who had. There was the cosy pub, run by the snobbish woman, the pensioner who lived alone with her cat, the young couple struggling to make ends meet, the local good-time girl looking a bit worn round the edges, the corner shop offering tick, and the bombastic old biddy across at the Mission Hall. An endless supply of stories, with rich characters.

Pardon the Expression came to an end in 1968 and I'm

afraid the last episode marred the whole experience for me. The script called for me to throw Arthur in a judo hold. In rehearsals I had no problem with this: I've always been agile so I was happy to do it, and the stunt arranger thought I'd be fine. They plotted the move so that Arthur came up behind me and put his arm around me then I reacted by bending down to grab his ankles so that he would end up flat on his back. Arthur didn't like the sound of that and insisted on us both standing on a mattress. That proved difficult for me because I had on high heels and the mattress wobbled. I said to Arthur, 'You must press against my back so that I know you're there,' but he said that idea was disgusting.

The show was recorded as live, and when it came to the scene he stood about a foot away from me so that when I bent down to find his ankles I had to stretch over and delve to find him. I felt my back click as I moved back into position although I wasn't bothered. I was annoyed with Arthur for being such a prude and not standing closer to me but I put it down to experience and left the show.

Six weeks later I decided to dry a little lace handkerchief by the fire. I bent down and fell on the floor. I was paralysed for eight weeks, in such agony that the doctors had to give me morphine. They had no idea what had happened. Eventually I regained the use of my legs and Freda took me to an osteopath, who was a great help. He discovered I'd put both my hips out of joint with my pelvic bone. I still have to have treatment for it and it's cost me thousands of pounds – all because Arthur Lowe wouldn't stand closer to me!

The injury left me on walking sticks and I decided the time had come to retire from the business. I'd had enough:

first my voice had gone, now my back. Mind you, I had no intention of remaining idle. I was only forty-eight and there was plenty of life left in me. Having been on the stage since I was twelve, Freda and I were at our best at night so we decided the best thing for us to do would be to run a pub – Freda had already had the experience of the failed country club. We sold the house and I bought a little pub in Derbyshire and became the licensee. You'll have to forgive me if I don't name it or give its location but, as you'll see, it was a strange place and I don't want to cause its present landlord any upset. Dad moved in with us and it became a family business. I had a great time on brewery courses, tapping barrels and pulling pints.

The problem with running a pub, though, was the smoky atmosphere, and my voice was getting lower and lower, and becoming very husky. Then one day in 1969 Harry Kershaw, the producer of *Coronation Street*, walked in and asked, 'Would you like to pull pints in the Rovers Return?'

I'd lost my professional nerve by then so I rushed into the kitchen to tell Freda and ask her advice. She said, 'Do you want to do it?' and I thought, Yes, yes, I do. I went and told Harry. However, there was a very big but, and I explained about my voice. I knew I'd really damaged it: I could hardly speak and singing a single note was impossible.

I went to see a throat specialist who said he could operate immediately to remove nodes from my vocal cords, which had been rubbing together for years, but that I wouldn't be able to speak at all for six weeks. Harry sorted out the contract and the next day I went into hospital. The next few weeks were a nightmare: I couldn't speak and the regulars in the pub kept trying to trick me into saying something.

They were laying bets to see who'd win. In the end Freda had to lecture them all and threaten to put a plaster over my mouth. After five weeks I was getting worked up as I was due to start on the *Street* at the beginning of the seventh week. That final week I was meant to learn how to speak again but I was terrified and the specialist had to coax my first words out of me.

So there I was, my voice a croaky little thing, deeper than it had been in the past, and feeling like a bag of nerves. I'd signed a year's contract to play Betty Turpin, sister of the *Street*'s shopkeeper Maggie Clegg, and married to a policeman. The night before I started rehearsals I sat with Freda and thought, What on earth have I let myself in for? Still, it was only for a year!

CHAPTER FOURTEEN

Betty 'Hotpot' Turpin

I thought I should give over a chapter of my autobiography to a woman I've known for the past thirty years, whose identity has become intertwined with my own. You know her as Betty, the jovial hotpot-making barmaid at the Rovers. I know her as a mask I slip on. Over the years the mask has moulded to my own face. I know where she ends and I begin, but it strikes me that the majority of *Coronation Street*'s viewers see the two Bettys as the same person.

Betty's full name at birth was Elizabeth Preston, and she was born three months before me, on 4 February 1920. Like me, she had a younger sister – Maggie – and a dominant parent. In Betty's case it was her father Harold, a tram inspector, who called the shots in the family home, 6 Tile Street, Weatherfield. He was a Bible-bashing Puritan and our Betty rebelled against him. Her mother, Margaret, was browbeaten and downtrodden. Betty left school to work as a cinema usherette at the Bijou, situated roughly where Audrey Roberts's hair salon now stands. Whilst I spent my war years entertaining munitions workers during *Workers' Playtime,* our Betty was one of the millions of lasses sitting at benches, singing along. She fell in love with a chap called Ted Farrell who returned to her after the war and courted her for a year before confessing he already had a wife. When he returned to his family he had no idea Betty was pregnant. Harold took charge and forced Betty to give away her baby son to be brought up by Maggie and her husband Les Clegg. Betty moved to Birmingham to live near the family and married Les's pal Cyril Turpin on 16 July 1949. Cyril was a policeman, and Betty enjoyed being a bobby's wife.

When she moved into *Coronation Street* in the summer of 1969, Betty was still married to Cyril. He'd transferred to Manchester as Betty wanted to be near Maggie, whose marriage to Les had ended in divorce. Maggie ran the Corner Shop on the Street, now owned by Dev Alahan, and Betty helped her out behind the counter as well as working at the bar of the Rovers Return. This Betty was a cheerful woman, fond of her food, and had won cups as a champion darts player. She was bossy, and hen-pecked Cyril – she could even out-gossip Hilda Ogden. To begin with, I can't say I was particularly fond of her.

When Harry Kershaw told me that Betty was going to be married I asked if Glenn Melvyn could play Cyril as we'd worked so well together in Blackpool. Unfortunately he was too ill to take the role and the part went to William Moore, a fine actor who was married to Mollie Sugden. Glenn was tall and thin and suited me because I was thick-set. Bill wasn't thin: his build was similar to mine and I don't think we looked good together on the screen. It's much easier to play a nagging wife when you're built like Flo and he's an Andy Capp! I enjoyed working with Bill but he would never touch me, which was hard to work round as we were meant to be married and should have given each other pecks on the cheek, or squeezed hands. It was because he had twin sons and he didn't want them to be confused or upset at seeing their father being intimate with another woman. I understood his reasoning but thought he was being daft: you can't be an actor and avoid intimate scenes.

Bill hated playing a copper and refused to wear the helmet – he used to carry it around under his arm. He was nervous too, and suffered a breakdown on the set. It happened during a scene in the Rovers and he couldn't remember his lines, perspiration poured off him and his face went blood red. They had to stop recording and he never finished the episode. That was the last time he appeared as Cyril; his character simply faded into the background and I played all my scenes in the Rovers and occasionally talked about how he was getting on. I was so pleased when Bill achieved fame in the eighties, playing the part of Father in the Ronnie Corbett show *Sorry*. I enjoyed working with him and have fond memories of him. He was a powerful healer: if anyone had a headache he'd put his hands near their head and you'd feel yourself getting better. Marvellous.

Coronation Street characters tend to fit into one of two camps: those who have drama after drama and those who muddle through life, often in the background, as sturdy and dependable as the famous cobbles. Betty falls into the latter group. Oh, there have been moments of drama, intrigue and even romance during her thirty years at the Rovers but it has been her presence behind the bar, cutting up pieces of lamb and chunks of potato, that has endeared her to the viewers.

In the early days Betty's stories revolved around her family. She plotted to buy into the Corner Shop, fancying herself behind the bacon-slicer, and was put out when sister Maggie refused to contemplate the idea of working with her day in and day out. Instead Betty stayed at the Rovers and was made senior barmaid by Annie Walker. A few years later Betty leant heavily on both Maggie and Annie when her beloved Cyril died of a heart attack whilst wheeling his bicycle out of the garage. She had a breakdown and became confused, wandering the streets calling his name. She had to be sedated and it looked as if she'd be too ill to attend his funeral but she rallied in time.

At the time of writing, Betty has attended eleven funerals and twelve weddings. Of the two, I think I prefer filming weddings: at least you tend not to get rained on. I'm dreadful at funerals. It's nerves. I always snigger and titter, just because I know I mustn't! I'll never forget filming Ernie Bishop's funeral in 1978. There we were, all dressed in black and looking mournful by an open grave, and there was Stephen Hancock, the actor who played Ernie, leaning against a gravestone eating a bacon sandwich while we were doing the shots. It was nearly impossible to stay sober.

After Maggie left England to live in Zaïre, the truth came out about Gordon really being Betty's son. She had to face him for the first time, admit that he was illegitimate and how she'd carried the stigma of his birth with her for years. She was delighted when Gordon told her she'd always been his favourite auntie and he was proud to have her as his mam. Since then Gordon has been an on-off visitor to the *Street*. He's married now, living in Wimbledon and prac-tising as a solicitor. His wife is called Caroline and he has a fifteen-year-old son called Peter. Betty's very proud of him.

I was surprised when the producer of the day, Susi Hush, told me that Gordon's birth certificate was going to be uncovered and it would be revealed that Betty was his real mother. The reason behind the story was that Irene Sutcliffe, the actress who played Maggie, had decided to leave the programme after six years and the writers wanted to keep the connection with Gordon. The story upset Irene terribly, as it wiped out the work she had put into the relationship with young Bill Kenwright. I had a lot of hate mail over that story, people calling me names as if I'd had the illegitimate son rather than my character. Bill's face is like mine and he could easily have been my son. By the time the story aired he was already a successful theatre producer and now I'm pleased to say his success knows no bounds. His shows are always on in the West End and all over the country and the world. I love him. He is the most thoughtful man. I get twelve roses sent to me every Valentine's Day and a bouquet on Mothering Sunday. Every time it happens I could weep.

Betty's had her fair share of romance: she might have been a widow but she was a merry one. To begin with, there was a fishmonger called Bert Gosling, but he was seen off by Annie Walker, who thought the whole salmon he slipped across the Rovers' bar was for her. For a time she was very friendly with Councillor Alf Roberts but nothing ever came of that, and then she had a regular ballroom dancing partner called George Daley. Then in 1980 came the startling revelation that she had received a marriage proposal sometime after Cyril had died but that she had turned down her suitor! Of course, she eventually walked down the aisle in 1995, when she married a wartime sweetheart, Billy Williams. They had a quick but traditional courtship, consisting of tea dances and walks in the park. All her family and friends came to the wedding but her happiness didn't last long. She lost husband number two to another heart attack, this time over his breakfast porridge.

Betty has always suffered misfortunes. In the late 1970s she hired Eddie Yeats to insulate her loft. Whilst in the house he invited in an old ex-con pal for a cuppa and when his back was turned the 'friend' swiped Betty's prized carriage clock. Of course, the clock was never found and soft-hearted Betty didn't pursue the matter with the police as she didn't want to get Eddie into trouble. That's typical of a Betty story: short and sweet, leaving you feeling sorry for her . . . ahhhh!

Betty has a soft spot for children, and she once reported a neighbour to the NSPCC for neglecting her kiddies – they were always out roaming the streets. The NSPCC sent an inspector round and warned the mother, and poor Betty was threatened by the woman's boyfriend, but the authorities assured her that she had done exactly the right thing.

She has not always lived alone at her semi in Hillside Crescent: pals such as Bet Lynch have slept in her spare bed, and she's also had lodgers, like Jerry Booth, young electrician Alec Hobson and a police sergeant called Tony Cunliffe, who took Bet and Rita Fairclough out at the same time. Of course, Betty didn't approve of behaviour like that and did a lot of tutting over the custard creams. Oh, she also has a cat, a lovely tabby called Marmaduke.

In 1982 she was brutally mugged whilst walking home, and ever since then has insisted on a taxi driving her to her door at night. Filming the mugging scene was one of the silliest things I've ever had to do: the director wanted me to walk along in the dark, cheerfully swinging my handbag, then disappear behind a wall and scream. I told him, 'I can't scream. Since I had my throat operation there's no way I can scream. I can shout but not scream.' So they got the assistant stage manager, a young girl, to scream. It was stupid. A thin little scream for this hefty piece! After the attack I had scenes in hospital and the makeup department did me proud. I had a great shiner over my eye. I looked like a panda! The incident was reported in the press and brought Ted Farrell visiting after nearly forty years. Betty was tempted to tell him about Gordon being his son but in the end decided least said, soonest mended, and kept him in the dark.

My worst moment acting in *Coronation Street* came in the chilly spring of 1983. The script called for Betty to go on an outing with Bet Lynch and Fred Gee. It was meant to be a lovely outing in the countryside, which was spoilt by the brakes failing on the car, sending it down a hill and into a lake. Betty and Bet were to be sitting in the car and end up water-logged. It was snowing, hailing and raining and we were supposed to be picnicking in Tatton Park for the May Bank Holiday. One bus got stuck in the mud trying to get the crew down to the edge of the water, the crane was bogged down and we needed tractors to drag the vehicles out of the mud. It was so soggy! It was a two-day shoot, and after reading the scripts I felt very apprehensive.

They took us there by coach and there were two women in wetsuits sitting at the back. I asked them what they were doing and they said, 'We're your stand-ins.' I said to Julie

Goodyear, 'Oh, kid, we're all right. Them women are going in for us.' We were so relieved because we'd both been dreading going into the lake.

After we arrived at Tatton we watched these women get into the car and we waited whilst the crew shoved the car into the lake, with them inside it. I said to Julie, 'Thank God we've not got to go in there.' They winched the car out on a tow rope and out these women got and started taking off their wet suits. I said, 'What are you doing?' They said they were just there to test that the car went in all right and we'd have to do the rest. I asked where our waterproofs were, because they said the water was freezing. The wardrobe lady said there were no wetsuits but I'd be all right because they had a pair of large navy blue waterproof trousers and a pair of big wellingtons for me to wear. I was the lucky one. All they had for Julie was a black bin bag, which she wore like a nappy.

We had to sit in the car, which was attached to a tractor by a tow-rope. The car rolled down the hill at a great speed then the tractor pulled and we were jolted to ensure the car landed in just the right spot. We nearly broke our necks and had awful whiplash. As soon as we hit the lake the water started to come into the car and we had to stay there, with that freezing water up to our waists. A stickleback swam in and was darting around me. We were both terrified. Poor Julie was only wearing a thin dress. Thankfully I had on a thick coat but it was still freezing. There was a swan swimming by and every time it passed the car window it hissed at us. I felt certain it was going to attack.

When it came to tea-break the director said there was no point in moving us so we were left. I was so indignant and started saying, 'I've been in this business fifty years and I've never been treated like this!' The only laugh in the whole experience was when I told Julie I needed to go to the toilet. She snorted, said she'd been ages ago and pointed out that we were in the middle of a huge lake and no one would notice what I did! It was awful. When we got back to the studio the producer, Mervyn Watson, had left a bottle of brandy in each of our dressing rooms with a note saying, 'Thank you, we asked you to do the impossible.' It *was* impossible. I would sooner be sacked than do anything like that again.

One of my happiest moments came in 1995 when Alf Roberts did Betty the honour of asking her to be his mayoress. She planted trees, opened community centres and old-folks' homes and drove around in a limo, loving every minute of it. When the time came for her to meet royalty, Audrey Roberts insisted on taking her place and the two bickered so much that Alf sent them to the function together, just for some peace and quiet.

Working in television can be glamorous at times, going to functions and meeting people you admire, but most of the time it's hard graft, involving long hours. Working on a stage play, you rehearse until it's perfect and then play the role time and time again so the words you say are second nature to you. In television you have hardly any rehearsals and have to be word-perfect straight away. As soon as your scene has been recorded you have to forget those lines and think about the ones you've yet to say. Location work is even worse than studio as you're at the mercy of the elements. In 1974 the story called for eight of us ladies to fly off to Majorca for a week's holiday. I can remember feeling quite excited at the prospect because it was a change in the schedule, something out of the ordinary. It was that, all right! It was *awful!* The beach was crawling with ants, the weather changeable and the hotel run-down. The director, Quentin Lawrence, was very strict. He used to stand in the swimming-pool in his little shorts and his camera and order the Germans who had paid for their holiday to get out of the pool and clear his shots. The hotel food was a disgrace and the makeup room was next to an open sewer. We had have to be up at seven a.m. but they wouldn't give us breakfast that early or even a cup of tea.

When we got back to Manchester the men sent us to Coventry. They wouldn't speak to us. Bernard Youens, who played Stan Ogden, said to me, 'It's all right for you lot. You've had a great time. We've been stuck here!'

Betty's time at the Rovers has been eventful: she's been sacked eight times, for incidents such as suspected theft, gossiping and being too old. She's walked out as well, over complaints about her cooking, frisky barmen, and once when Fred Gee overstepped the mark and remarked on the size of her bottom. But she's always returned: it's a second home to her. Landlords and landladies come and go but Betty remains, dishing out the hotpot along with comforting words.

She doesn't do many evening shifts now and concentrates on lunchtime work. I'm not sure how long she'll remain at the pub. Alec Gilroy used to refer to her as Mother Hubbard, or the Oldest Barmaid in Town. Who knows if she'll still be pulling pints in her nineties? I certainly don't!

And finally, for the thousands of people who've written in for the recipe, here is Betty's famous hotpot!

BETTY'S HOTPOT

1½lb (675g) neck of lamb, cubed
1½lb (675g) potatoes, peeled and thinly sliced
1 large or 2 medium onions, roughly chopped
¾ pint (425ml) light stock or hot water
1 tablespoon Worcestershire sauce
1 bay leaf
1 tablespoon flour
1oz (25g) dripping and 1oz (25g) butter
or 2oz (50g) butter
salt and pepper to season

1. Preheat the oven to 170°C/325°F/gas mark 5. Melt the dripping or 1oz (25g) butter over a high heat in a heavy-bottomed frying pan until the fat smokes. Seal the meat and continue frying until nicely browned. Remove the pieces from the pan to a deep casserole or divide among four individual high-sided, ovenproof dishes. Turn down the heat to medium. Fry the onions in the pan juices, adding a little more butter or dripping if necessary. When the onions are soft and starting to brown, sprinkle on the flour and stir in to soak up the fat and juices. As the flour paste starts to colour, start adding stock or water a few tablespoons at a time, stirring vigorously to avoid lumps. Gradually add the rest of the liquid and bring to a simmer, stirring continuously, add the Worcestershire sauce and season to taste.

2. Pour the onions and liquid over the meat and mix well. Add the bay leaf. Arrange the potatoes over the meat in overlapping layers, seasoning each layer. Dot the top layer with the remainder of the butter.

3. Cover the dish and place on the top shelf of the oven for 2 hours. Uncover and cook for a further 30 minutes. If the potatoes are not brown by this point, turn up the oven and cook for a further 15 minutes, or finish off under the grill, brushing the potato slices with more butter if they look too dry.

CHAPTER FIFTEEN

My Friends on the Street

I started work on *Coronation Street* in May 1969 and my first episode was broadcast on 2 June. My first scene, entering the Corner Shop, introduced me as Betty Turpin, the bossy older sister of Maggie Clegg, shop proprietor. It was played thus:

EPISODE 881, SCENE 5

INTERIOR: CORNER SHOP

BETTY: So, this is your famous Corner Shop?

MAGGIE: It makes a nice little living.

BETTY: I can see that, pet. Ohhh and the way you've got it all set out! As methodical as ever! Eh, remember what our mam used to call you? Methodical Mag.

MAGGIE: Yeah, and I remember what she used to call you as well!

BETTY: We'll have none of that! You'll have me chucked out, tarred and feathered before

I've even set foot in the district! Eh, what are
they like round here?
MAGGIE: The neighbours? Or the customers?
BETTY: Well . . . both.
MAGGIE: Mixed . . . you know. The people in this street
are all right, once you get to know them.

Before my first episode was over I had been taken on as
barmaid at the Rovers Return and it was there that I met my
first friend on the programme. Betty was employed by landlord Jack Walker, in the absence of his wife Annie. Jack was
played by veteran actor Arthur Leslie, a wonderful, sensitive
man who had run his own repertory company after the war.
He was so warm-hearted and was the cornerstone of the
show, providing advice for nervous young actors and a
calming influence for us nervous older ones.

I have to say, I was completely and utterly petrified of
joining the show. It had been running since December
1960, and since May 1961 had seldom been off the number-
one spot in the ratings. It drew audiences of eight million
and the cast were treated like royalty wherever they went. I'd
been used to stardom but this was beyond that: I was joining
a phenomenon. Arthur was the most calming influence on
me. The operation to my throat just weeks before had left
me feeling I would not be able to utter a sentence, but
Arthur took me under his wing. 'Come on, Betty,' he said,
'your only scenes are with me and whenever you have to say
a line you'll feel my hand on the small of your back.' I
worked for about a fortnight and every scene I did I had
Arthur's hand on my back, giving me confidence. I'll never
forget him for that: he was just like a guardian angel.

Making an episode of *Coronation Street* was different thirty years ago from what it is today. In those long-off days of glorious black and white, the show was transmitted twice a week, on Mondays and Wednesdays, at seven thirty p.m. The cast were a tight-knit bunch of seventeen – I wonder how many character names you can remember from when I first appeared? The layout of the Street looked like this:

Rovers Return	Jack and Annie Walker, paying guests Lucille Hewitt and Emily Nugent
No.1	Albert Tatlock
No.3	Dickie and Audrey Flemming
No.5	Minnie Caldwell and her cat Bobby
No.7	(didn't exist: there was a bench in the gap)
No.9	Len Fairclough and Ray Langton
No.11	Elsie Tanner
No.13	Stan and Hilda Ogden
Corner Shop	Maggie Clegg

Opposite the terrace stood maisonettes occupied by Ena Sharples, and Ken and Val Barlow.

Seventeen names, many etched now in the annals of television history. Nowadays we have forty-five regular cast members.

In a modern episode of *Coronation Street* a third of the scenes are shot on location, in parks, hospitals or schools; in the *Street* of 1969 the odd scene was shot on the exterior *Street* location, but that was it. All the action took place inside the terraced homes and meeting places. Our week would start with long rehearsals in a huge room where masking tape on the floor denoted walls and doorways and chipped furniture stood in for tables and sideboards. We'd rehearse holding our scripts, moving to where we were directed and writing down notes. Once the director was happy with the content we'd do a run-through of both episodes in front of the producer. That tended to take place on the Wednesday afternoon. We then broke until the Thursday afternoon when we'd gather in costume and makeup to record the scenes on camera. Editing time was a precious commodity in those days, so the scenes had to be recorded in chronological order. Not live, but 'as live'. This meant that if you made a mistake you just carried on because if you stopped everyone had to go back to the beginning and record it all again. You tended to find that fluffs at the start of an episode were easily forgiven but those in the closing scenes brought down the wrath of sixteen other actors on your head! Thursday afternoons and all day Friday were for recording the two episodes. I say all day Friday, but in reality as soon as the director was happy that he'd recorded it all we could go home.

What a difference today! At the time of writing we make four episodes a week and our schedule is run like a military operation. Sundays is location work, at Fresco's supermarket, or Weatherfield General Hospital. Monday we film on the Street lot, all those little scenes coming out of houses and driving down the cobbles. Tuesday we block the interior scenes – this means standing in the sets, which normally means the Rovers for me, and being told by the director where to stand and where to walk to. The rest of the working week (seven a.m. Wednesday through to Friday seven p.m.) consists of recording all the interior scenes.

Editing has taken over and now we no longer have to do everything in story order. I am usually called in for two of the three days to record all my scenes in any order, with the main dramatic two-handers, such as Deirdre and Ken scenes, being recorded one after the other on the third day. Each director works in a different way. Rehearsal time goes out of the window but thankfully we all know our stuff and most of us rise to the challenge of learning lines and positions, then getting on with it ourselves. After thirty years I think I know Betty's motivation pretty well! Scenes are either recorded all in one go or the director will cut them down into little segments and edit them together a week later. So very different, but we can't live in the past, can we?

A few months after I started in *Coronation Street* word of it must have reached South Africa, because Wally phoned and said, 'Hello, baby, where did we go wrong?' He said he was in England and wanted me to 'pop on the train down to London so we could spend the weekend together'. The cheek of the man! I said, 'If there's any "popping" to do, it would be you getting on a train and "popping" up here, but don't bother "popping" because my father will be on our front step with the carving knife.' That was the last time I heard from him but the sound of his voice sent shivers down my spine. He was my unfinished business and I felt threatened just knowing he was still around. Dad insisted that I got a divorce, because otherwise Wally would have a claim on my *Street* earnings. Thankfully he didn't contest it. As I stood in the divorce court I felt like a prostitute. The judge asked me if I'd slept with any men since leaving my husband then asked Freda whether she knew if I'd cohabited with any men. It was outrageous, hurtful too. The judge eventually granted the divorce on the grounds that Wally had deserted me. On paper, at least, I'd been married for sixteen years.

I didn't know the *Street* cast when I started, apart from Pat Phoenix, who'd hung around me that time in Blackpool, and Eileen Derbyshire, who played Emily Nugent and quickly became a firm friend. I'm pleased to say our friendship is still as strong as it was thirty years ago. I love recording scenes with Eileen, although we both have this terrible problem: we can't have photographs taken with each another. It's practically impossible. As soon as we look at each other she goes hysterical and I start to cry with laughter. The photographer always thinks we're mad. The last picture we had taken I said, 'It's no good, I can't look at her face and she can't look at me without laughing,' so Granada's stills photographer, Neil Marland, told me to look at one wall and Eileen to look at another. At least they got a picture.

At some point in the early seventies Eileen and I set off together to splash out on furs. I know it's not politically correct nowadays but then *everyone* had furs. I'd got my first fur when I was eighteen. My parents bought me a string of lovely sables – with my money – but I hadn't bought any more and Eileen had none. It was Doris Speed who pushed us into it: 'Now then, girls, you're in an important programme, you have to look the part. If you do personal appearances the public don't want to see you in tweed or a raincoat. They expect mink.' She kept on at us for so long that one lunch-time Eileen and I went into town to Kendal's, the huge department store, and up to the fur department. The shop assistant looked us up and down, sneered as if we were a nasty smell or a couple of whores, and asked, 'Is there anything I can do to help you?'

I said, 'Yes. We require two classic coats in dark mink.' She went away, came back with a grey mink and forced Eileen into it, ignoring me. I said, 'We want two, classic dark minks.'

To look good, mink has to hang down and the coat she forced on Eileen was cut so that the pelts ran across and not down. She looked like the Michelin man. I told her to take it off. Again, I told the assistant what we wanted, and again she took no notice, this time bringing out a palomino coat. I complained so she pointed at me and said, 'You, sit there!' Eileen was nearly in tears as this woman kept bringing her the most unsuitable coats. This woman said to her, 'The thing is, you're such a funny shape and you,' looking at me 'you're too fat!' I just sat there, thinking I'd hit her if I stood up. She glared at me and said, 'I'll tell you now, there's nothing in this shop that'll fit you.' I grabbed hold of Eileen and we marched out. I was so angry that I phoned the manager and cancelled the account I'd had there since I was fifteen. We had been prepared to spend up to two thousand pounds each on mink. He was deeply apologetic and begged me not to, but I was so cross. There's no need for anyone to be rude and I hate rudeness.

I still have lots of my furs. I have a full-length black mink coat, a silver mink three-quarter coat, three mink stoles and a palomino short jacket. I haven't worn them for twenty years. They're hanging in my wardrobe. When I bought them I had no idea how they were bred, and now I wouldn't consider wearing them. But I just can't part with them.

Doris Speed, who played Rovers Return landlady Annie

Walker from 1960 to 1983, was a lovely woman. When I joined the programme she was one of the *Street*'s biggest stars. When the show began in 1960 she'd just retired from her job as PA to one of the big bosses at Guinness. Years of amateur dramatics had taught her how to appreciate the fame she achieved and she was not impressed at all to have a *variety* actress in her show. She made no bones about looking down on me. That was in the beginning, though. Once she realized I wasn't so bad she mellowed towards me and we became great friends.

What can I tell you about Doris? She was a gentle lady, a quiet soul who lived with her mother. She didn't suffer fools but was generous and kind-hearted. I'll never forget one scene I played with her. Betty's husband Cyril had just died and Annie had called round to offer words of condolence, one widow to another. We sat on a couch all dressed in mourning black. I could tell she was troubled by something, and eventually she asked if I was going to move at all during the scene. I said I wasn't so she produced her script, cut up into a long strip and pinned it all down my arm and my thigh! I had to sit perfectly still so that the camera wouldn't pick up the pieces of paper. She said it was the only way she was going to get through the scene. Years later Fred Feast, who played barman Fred Gee, wanted to pin his lines to my back but I wouldn't let him. I know we sometimes have pages and pages of lines to memorize but I think actors should be able to learn them. Maybe I'm being insensitive: I've always been lucky enough to learn lines with no problems – I'm a quick study.

Margot Bryant was a little tinker. She played timid Minnie Caldwell. Remember her? Ena Sharples's pal who wouldn't say boo to a goose? Well, in real life she swore like a trooper! She and Doris were at each other's throats all the time. Doris was staunch Labour and Margot was Tory. My problem was that I was friends with both of them and used to get caught in the crossfire. I'll never forget the night Freda and I took them both to Oldham Rep to see a production of *Arsenic and Old Lace*. It was directed by Bill Roache, the *Street*'s Ken Barlow, and also starred Jean Alexander and Bernard Youens (Stan and Hilda Ogden). Peter Dudley was in it, years before being cast as Bert Tilsley, and he stole the show. Jean played one of the two homicidal old ladies, Bunny the mad uncle, Bryan Mosley was a policeman and Bill took the lead.

Both Doris and Margot had asked Freda and me to take them so we ended up going together, with casting director Jose Scott. The only seats I could get were in the back row of the circle and as soon as we sat down Margot started grumbling about the poor view and the terrible seats. Doris was hissing loudly across me at Margot to shut up. Margot ignored her and started on at the woman in front of her who was wearing a hat. 'I hope that bloody hat's coming off!' said Margot.

The woman turned round and said, 'I am not removing my hat.'

Margot said, 'I'm gonna knock that bloody hat off her head!' She went on and on, and Doris and I sank into our seats because everyone was glaring at us. In the end Jose and Doris went to stand in the aisle to get away from her.

The performance was dire. It was the worst piece of theatre I'd ever seen. Jean played it all in her mouse character: she was the quiet sister so she brought her hands up a lot to her face, as if she were nibbling something. Bunny had to keep racing up and down a flight of stairs with a trumpet. He had a bottle of whisky at the foot of the stairs and another at the top and he'd take swigs from each bottle. They had mattresses behind the staircase in case he fell off. He was drunk for half of the play. Our cast shouldn't have done it. It was foreign to them.

Margot left the show in 1976 and for the last year or so of her time as Minnie she was something of a headache for me. I used to give her lifts in my car and she started ordering me about as if I was a chauffeur and treated the car as if it were hers. The Government were talking about bringing back petrol rationing so finally I said I couldn't take her home any more as it was right out of my way and I was wasting so much petrol. She was furious that she had to use a taxi, and after that not a day went by without her telling me how much she'd had to pay for it. 'Two pounds today!' When she stopped acting she went to live in a nursing home, and Freda and I often visited but it was always an uphill struggle with her: she used to row so much! Eventually we told the sister we weren't coming any more. Then I received a phone call from the home and this irate woman shouted that we were awful for abandoning her, as if we were her daughters. I said, 'I'm sorry, but she's not a relative. We just used to work together.' But the caller said we had been her only visitors.

The *Street*'s battleaxe, Ena Sharples, was played by wonderful Violet Carson, who lived in Blackpool with her sister Nellie. Freda and I have many happy memories of them both. I never met a more elegant lady than Vi Carson. I adored her. As she got older she became introverted and pessimistic and thought people were against her. Pre-*Street*,

I had met her on several occasions whilst she had been working with Wilfred Pickles on the wireless but I didn't have much to do with her as she was just an accompanist. After years of admiring her as foul-tongued Ena, wearing that horrible old raincoat and hairnet, I was astounded to discover how refined she was when I joined the *Street*. Her image on the screen didn't appeal to me at all; it was so grubby. In real life she was elegant, very smart. I wish people today in showbusiness would dress nicely and behave as we used to behave. I was born into a beautiful, glamorous profession, but not many people treat it with the same respect now which saddens me.

Away from the *Street*, Freda and I were far from inactive. We still ran the pub in Derbyshire with Dad. After pulling pints at the Rovers I'd return home to pull more, although Freda did most of the work. The hotel was old, steeped in history, and we soon discovered that odd things happened there. I bought some beautiful tropical fish and put them in a tank on the bar. The next morning they were all dead. We had parakeets which we decided to bring down from our living quarters and keep in the bar. At four o'clock every day they'd start to screech uncontrollably and within a week all their feathers had fallen out. Our boxer dog, Adam, hated the pub, and we used to hear voices asking for drinks when it was closed and there were just the three of us in the place. We'd have a game of darts before opening up and you'd hear someone say, 'Pull us a pint, Fred,' and no one would be there.

Whilst we were at the pub Dad fell very ill. The doctor told us he had lung cancer and needed constant nursing. I was working at the studios and Freda had the pub to deal with so I insisted he went to hospital. He was there for two weeks before he died. He never forgave me for sending him away and not letting him die in his own bed. We visited him every day and saw him fade away almost before our eyes. It was shattering to watch – and I felt so guilty. But there had been no alternative. I felt even more wretched when he'd kiss Freda and talk to her but ignore me. When he died, we were relieved that he was out of his pain, but we missed him. At least over the last few years which he'd lived with us we'd made up for some of the time my mother had kept us apart from him when we were children.

At the pub Freda did all the cellarwork and her beer was renowned. People came for miles to sample it: Freda had it sparkling like diamonds. One day she was in the cellar tilting a barrel when a tapping mallet lifted itself off its hooks on a wall and flung itself round a corner and straight at her head. Luckily she saw it coming and dodged it. In the bar we had a cigarette-card display case cemented to the wall. One night, whilst we were serving it wrenched itself off the wall and flew about ten feet at Freda. A customer saw it coming and called out, and again she wasn't hurt, just shaken. One night I woke up at four o'clock and smelt cigar smoke. I went to the top of the stairs and heard voices in the bar, as if people were playing cards and smoking. But no one was there. We had another fish tank, filled it with fish and, once again, overnight, the fish died. The final straw was when a bottle on a glass shelf behind the bar started to dance all by itself then jumped into the air and threw itself straight at Freda's legs. She was agile and jumped but I couldn't put up with this any longer. The next day I phoned the brewery and asked to have the place exorcized. They refused, so I gave notice. Within the month we'd moved out to take on the tenancy of the Devonshire Arms in Mellor, near Marple, a lovely quiet pub in the country.

We ran the Devonshire for two years but Freda was tied to it, and I was exhausted after working in the studio all day. Eventually we decided we'd had enough and considered moving. Freda picked up the local paper and there, staring out at us, were the details of a little farmhouse for sale: Snape Hay Farm, Cobden Edge. It was pouring with rain but we got the car out and drove up to it. Cobden Edge is a thousand feet above sea level and the farm was remote. It was surrounded in mist and I refused to get out of the car, telling Freda I wasn't interested. However, the next day it was fine and it looked completely different: a beautiful little farmstead. We knocked on the door and asked to view. A lady showed us round and was a bit startled when, as soon as we had set foot inside the door, we told her we'd buy it. It was beautiful. As well as the house there were plenty of outhouses, which would convert into kennels, a pigsty, a barn and an acre of paddock. We paid £11,150 for it and seventeen years later I sold it for £120,000!

The hill was a 1 in 2 gradient and in winter it was murder to get out of the house. One winter, in 1982, we woke up early as I had to get to the studios and there were five-foot-high snowdrifts against the house. There was no way I could get the car out so I phoned the producer, Bill Podmore, and told him I was stuck. He said not to worry and that he'd send a helicopter from Leeds for me. Freda had to go into the field next to the farm and test where the ground was level enough for the helicopter to land. Then, when we heard it coming, she had to stand in the field and direct it with a tea-towel. Of course, Granada was intent on making as much publicity out of this as possible so there was a film crew in the 'copter and a journalist turned up after walking on top of the walls, through the snow. He was frozen when he arrived and we warmed him up with brandy. Then the helicopter pilot felt he couldn't land so I was told to stand by to be winched! I said, 'You can cut that out! There's no way I'm being winched!' By this time the village was awake and everyone was out watching. Thankfully it landed and I was flown to Barton airport in ten minutes. It took a car over an hour to drive me from there to the studios. After that I told Freda we'd have to move. I couldn't go through anything like that again.

We moved to a house in Hale Barns, Cheshire, and stayed there for five years, and now we live in an apartment in a refurbished Georgian mansion in Bowdon, near Altrincham, Cheshire. It was darling Thelma Barlow, the *Street*'s dithering Mavis Riley, who first introduced us to Altrincham. She joined *Coronation Street* in 1973 and we got on like a house on fire immediately. She's a very private, educated lady, with a wonderful sense of humour and, really, she's the only member of the cast with whom Freda and I have ever socialized. Whenever it was snowing in the winter and I had an early call I'd stay at her house and play with her sons James and Clive. Thelma now lives in Yorkshire and has a beautiful rural garden that Freda and I helped to landscape. I was very sad when she left the show in 1997 and miss her terribly.

A year after joining the *Street* I was reunited with dear Jack Watson, my wartime sweetheart. He came into the show to play Chief Petty Officer Bill Gregory, who proposed marriage to Elsie Tanner. It was wonderful to see him again. When he arrived I was so excited. He still looked sensational and had a few film roles under his belt. Of course he was married and had three children, but he was still my Jack and I felt like a giggling schoolgirl as soon as I read in my script that he was going to be in it. We did a scene together in the pub and he stopped rehearsals and told everyone, 'I nearly married this lady. She was my very first love.' I was so embarrassed but he refused to shut up and carried on in front of everyone! But having him there upset me deeply too. I couldn't stop thinking of what might have been instead of what had been. He'd have made a wonderful husband.

Jack appeared three times as Bill Gregory, first in the early sixties, then in 1970 and, finally, in 1983, when he was brought back to drag Elsie off to live in Portugal with him. That was when Pat Phoenix left the show for good. She'd already left once before, in 1973, when she and her then husband Alan Browning, who played her screen husband Alan Howard, left to pursue theatre work. I went to see a couple of their plays. The first was *Subway in the Sky*. Pat opened in it just before leaving the *Street*. I think she was dipping her toe in the water, feeling her way. The production was in Wilmslow, at the Rex Theatre. I went with Freda and Barbara Knox and we sat in the row in front of Harry Kershaw and the then producer Eric Prytherch. It was an awful play – the men went to the bar during the interval and never returned!

At the end we wanted to go home but Pat knew we were in the audience so we had to go backstage. We had to wait for a while because Pat wanted to prepare herself. We found her in a négligée with ostrich feathers down it, reclining on a *chaise-longue*. I didn't know what to say. Barbara had only recently joined as a permanent member of the cast, as singer and newsagent Rita Littlewood. Pat took one look at Barbara, waved a finger at her and said, 'I know what your bloody game is! You've come into my show and you think you can oust me! Well, you can bloody well think again!' Poor Barbara hadn't even opened her mouth. 'I've been told all about you!' Pat said.

Freda and I just stood there, feeling embarrassed for Barbara whilst Pat's insecurities tumbled out. After a while Pat acknowledged that we were also in the room and asked me what I'd thought of the show. All I could think of to say was 'Well, you worked very hard.' She pulled a face and said, 'It's bloody awful, isn't it?' She wasn't a fool. She did another play, *Gaslight*, and was very good in that, but I have to say that the best performance I've seen a *Street* actor give on stage was by Barbara Knox in Neil Simon's *Gingerbread Lady*. She was sensational. To my mind she's one of the best dramatic actresses in the business. She's certainly the strongest one in our show and I'm very fond of her.

Going back to Pat, I'll never forget some of the most wonderful car journeys I've ever had in my life. When I lived in Derbyshire, Pat didn't live far away and I used to give her lifts to and from work. I'd pick her up and, after exchanging pleasantries, I'd get her to tell me a play or a poem. And on every journey she'd bring a play to life for me, so I could picture it all. She'd done so many plays in rep and would recall them for me in detail. It got so that she'd bring books of poetry for the hour-long journey and read them to me in her beautiful voice.

Pat was only ever bitchy to people when she felt threatened by them. She was one of the kindest people I've ever met. Her death from lung cancer in 1986 was a hard blow to us all. In keeping with her personality, though, her funeral was quite something. She didn't want anyone to be miserable and we were told not to wear black. The priest concluded the service, and then it was as if she'd raised the coffin lid and said, 'Right, now let's have some fun.' The brass band started playing 'When The Saints Come Marching In'. She went out as she wanted to go, bless her.

The *Street* is known for its strong female characters but some of the longest-serving cast members have been men. William Roache, who plays Ken Barlow, has been around for forty years: he appeared in the very first episode. He is a close friend of mine and I'm godmother to his son William while Freda is godmother to his daughter Verity. He's a good-thinking person, kind and generous. I adore working with him and spending time with his family. His first wife was Anna Cropper, who I rate very highly as an actress and, of course, their son Linus is now a respected film and Shakespearean actor.

Another long-serving actor was dear Bryan Mosley who played Alf Roberts for thirty-six years. He was a fine man, and enveloped you with his warmth. The Salford artist Harold Riley once gave me a painting he'd done of the Pope blessing a child. (A copy of it can be seen at the Hidden Gem, a delightful Catholic church in Manchester's city centre.) It hung in our hallway for years and then, when Bryan was ill, we felt he would get so much more out of it than us as he was a Catholic. I was overwhelmed by how much that painting meant to him. Just before he died he wrote me a note, full of warmth and love. He always said that to him I was the only true 'star' in the *Street* as he'd come to see me in his youth and had bought my records. He was a lovely, modest man and I miss him.

Being part of the *Street* family is sometimes very sad. Graham Haberfield, who played brickie Jerry Booth, was a much-loved cast member, and when he died of a heart attack in his thirties in 1975 we were all shattered. I'll never forget his funeral: we were given the afternoon off work and a coach drove us to the cemetery where he was to be buried. The press were out in force, trampling over the graves to click us as we cried, and I remember little Helen Worth breaking down. I was wearing a large mink coat and I embraced her in it, hiding her and telling her to cuddle me. She still reminds me about that, all these years later. I've always loved Helen. She joined the cast in 1974 as Gail Potter and in the show has been married, divorced, remarried, widowed, married yet again and has three children. But back in the seventies Gail was still a daft-headed teenager, living above the Corner Shop with her mate Tricia, played by Kathy Jones. Those two girls were my little babies. I adored them and mothered them. Kathy left the show in 1976 and furthered her career as a singer, presenting the children's programme *Handful of Songs* for Granada. She had a wonderful voice but tragically she had to give it all up because singing so much in front of groups and music systems cost her her hearing. She and Helen were just the most wonderful girls. I'd go up to them and say, 'Come and give your mother a big kiss!' I still do with Helen. I wrap my arms around her and hold her close. She brings out my mothering instincts.

The ensemble 'feel' within the cast is very important. I've watched people like Helen and Anne Kirkbride grow up on the show. Annie was just eighteen when she started as Deirdre Hunt and I've watched her flourish and eventually become happy. She wasn't happy for a long time and was terribly lonely, always looking for Mr Right. Freda once advised her to stop searching for happiness, saying it would find her. And it did. When David Beckett joined the cast to play Deirdre's new fella, Dave Barton, their eyes met in the Green Room and that was that! She said, 'I did what you and Freda said, I stopped looking!' They're a lovely couple and I was thrilled when they married. She's a homemaker and loves her home life. She's a shopaholic, too, and given any excuse she goes off to Kendal's and comes back weighed down with bags and parcels. I always make her show me what she's bought. I get her to spread everything out in the Green Room and show it to me, like a child at Christmas.

These girls, I've watched them day after day, seeing them grow up, and I've come home to Freda and talked about them. We've worried over them for years, while they've gone through relationships and hard times. In a spiritual way I try and help them just by watching and loving them. I'm proud of them, very proud.

Another girl I adore, although not of the same generation, is Sarah Lancashire, who joined the *Street* as Raquel in 1991 and left five years later. She was a joy to work with, and when she left the Rovers, well, for me a light went out and it's never been the same since. When I heard she was leaving I was so upset. Everything she did was right. She never missed a line or an inclination. She's a clever girl and I admire her no end.

I feel lost if I do a scene in the Kabin or the Corner Shop. I feel that I want to get behind the counter. The Rovers is my set. I'm totally familiar with it and the props. Mind you, it's a terrible set to work in, very tiring because it kills your back, your knees and your feet. You get new actresses coming to work behind the bar and they have high heels on and I smirk at them and wait, and by the end of the first week they're in flat-heeled shoes and look worn out.

I love working with actors such as Eileen and Barbara because I can relax, knowing how they work and feeling 100 per cent sure everything's going to be all right. With new people I get nervous because they may not work as I work. I'm used to going through scenes time and time again. The younger ones don't seem to do that so often: they learn as they go along. Jane Danson, who plays Leanne, is a very conscientious girl and she always knows her lines perfectly. But she's one of many, and nowadays youngsters come and go so quickly that you can't keep up with them all.

As I've said, I have great long-standing friendships with those who I've worked with since the early Seventies but the wonder of *Coronation Street* is that new, talented actors are always joining us. Ian Mercer has a marvellous quality in his humility. He plays Gary Mallett wonderfully and the scenes following his screen wife's death took my breath away. He handles Gary's two children beautifully. I could look at him for hours. He has wonderfully honest eyes. And, of course, David Neilson is sensational as Roy Cropper, incredibly talented, a man who deserves many awards as, so carefully, he puts on the mask to play Roy. He's a lovely, eccentric man with a sharp eye for detail and underplays each scene so well. When the record light goes on in studio Ian and David are two of the few who don't stiffen. They're both very loose and laid-back.

Bill Tarmey is a love. Jack Duckworth is one of my all-time favourite characters. I just wish Bill would stop smoking. I worry about him and his health all the time. He is such a marvellous family man, so in love with his wife Alli and his kids. He does everything in the world for them. He's kind all the way through and a generous actor. I miss having him behind the Rovers bar.

In the seventeen years he's been in the *Street* Kevin Kennedy has come on leaps and bounds and has made a niche for himself as Curly Watts. I think he's like a breath of fresh air. He's lovely. He's turned Curly into a warm, understanding character. He's come out of the wilderness and he's better playing straight than comedy. I may be biased but I think our actors are the best. Simply the best.

Over the years many of my stories were set around troubles behind the Rovers bar and most of my scenes were played with Julie Goodyear, who played Bet Lynch Gilroy from 1970 until 1995. Twenty-five years, and I'm pleased to say we never had a cross word. Never! When she joined I said to her, 'I'll never have a row with you. I don't like rowing and if we have a row I'll leave the show.' She agreed with me that if ever we were upset over something the other had done we'd talk about it and clear the air. She was wonderful to work with, professional to the core. She has a great sense of humour. If she could have kept her sense of humour going on-screen as she does off-screen she would have been a riot, but when the record light went on you'd see the stomach go in, the bust come out, and she hardened herself to become Bet. We worked perfectly together, which was something of a miracle.

And did we have a laugh behind that bar! I remember one scene in which we had to stand at the back and gradually walk down to the pumps. The director, Quentin Lawrence, rang a fire bell before going for a shot so everyone would be quiet. But it was his first time with us and he didn't warn us about the bell. He just said he didn't want us to camp it up – no little expressions, no Lancashire speak, just delivered as it was written. Then he let the fire bell off and we both nearly jumped out of our skins. I thought I was going to have a heart attack. Julie's eyes went pink and I was sweating. I couldn't think of my lines or my moves or anything. He'd put the fear of God into us. Julie realized I'd lost it so she said my line then I said hers, and we carried on with the entire scene like that, doing one another's lines. When we finished we were soaking wet with terror and he came up to us and said, 'Now, that's how I want it in future!'

Another time, we were standing at the back by the till and they'd painted the bar floor because they were going to take a shot of our feet. If you drop any liquid on to paint in studio it becomes like glue and this happened as we spilt some beer. When we tried to walk we couldn't move; our shoes were stuck firm. This was when we filmed every scene as if it was live so we both had to step out of our shoes and do the scene in our stockinged feet.

One of the funniest things Julie and I did was appear as Laurel and Hardy. The men had beaten the ladies at bowls and the losers had to put on a cabaret in drag. When Wardrobe brought in the costumes I nearly died! I had never seen so many fly-buttons on trousers before. We shared a dressing room and I was struggling so much to do them up that Julie's little son Gary had to crawl between my legs to do them for me. Wardrobe padded me up and pulled all the excess trouser up behind me. I had a little tash to wear but I've always perspired on my face terribly. Julie and I had to do this song-and-dance routine on a stage in the pub. My tash wouldn't stay on and whenever I said anything it flew off. Julie was uncontrollable. We couldn't keep straight faces at all! The director said, 'If you two don't behave yourselves I'll order you out of the studio and out of the building!' I shall never know, to this day, how we got those shots in.

Costume can cause so many problems. I'm pleased I've not had to have a trademark item, like Hilda's rollers or Bet's earrings. My clothes mainly come from Marks and C&A. They used to come from the market but I got a new wardrobe when we went to colour in 1969. When that happened they did screen tests with us to match our colourings. They didn't want us clashing on the screen. With me having brown hair they bought me a brown frock with long puffed sleeves in a thin material with big yellow and orange flowers on it. They hung it in my dressing room and I said to Jean Alexander, 'Good God! I've not got to wear that, have I?' It was hideous brown Crimplene. I wore it about four times then refused to put it on any more. And I got hundreds and hundreds of letters asking where it had come from and why I wasn't wearing it. I couldn't believe anyone would like that dress. In the end I sent it to one of the fans. The same thing happened to Eileen Derbyshire. She always had a plastic handbag that was stamped like crocodile skin. She had dozens of letters saying, 'How could a person like Emily Bishop possibly buy such a magnificent handbag?' Eventually she stopped using it and got Wardrobe to parcel it up and send it to one of the correspondents.

For twenty years I shared a dressing room with Jean Alexander, the *Street*'s Hilda Ogden, and in our spare time we used to make padded coat-hangers for charity. We'd sit in our dressing room surrounded by coat-hangers and sold them to the rest of the cast. Barbara would buy a dozen, Julie would. All the money used to go to the Queen Elizabeth Hospital in Birmingham where they were collecting for a scanner. I'd buy the hangers and we'd scrounge material from people and sit there padding and sewing. We sold hundreds. Jean would cut out the material and I sewed.

I'll never forget a trip I took with Jean and the rest of the cast in 1970. To celebrate the thousandth episode of the *Street*, *TV Times* took us all to Belle Vue, a famous northern zoo and amusement park, to photograph us on the rides and looking at the animals in the zoo. Jean and I went off on our own to find the big cats. There was a gorgeous Bengal tiger in an enclosure, lying in the sun. We both stood there looking at it and it got up and came towards us. Then it turned its back on us, lifted its tail and sprayed us both. All over our faces and shoulders. We were soaked and the smell was appalling. When we got back to the coach they wouldn't let us on as we stank so much. They made us sit on the back row with the windows wide open. I picked up my car from the studios and drove home. When I got to the door Freda refused to let me in and I had to get undressed outside in the dark before she'd let me in for a bath. We had to fumigate the car!

The cast of *Coronation Street* once performed a special stage show for a Royal Command Performance at

Manchester's Palace Theatre. John Stevenson wrote the script and thankfully I didn't have much to say in it. Jean and Violet Carson had most of the lines and they were both terrified. Vi's background was radio, Jean's was rep and they hadn't played to such a large audience before. The Palace is a large musical stage, and Jean had to stand on there in her curlers shouting, 'Stanleeeeeeeeee!' and wheeling him off on a porter's trolley. She was so frightened I didn't think she'd make it. I tried to calm her and said I'd stand on the side of the stage and prompt if she forgot lines, but she was fine.

It all went off well, but at the end we had to line up at the footlights and say things to the audience. I was standing between Vi and Doris. Vi was petrified. I got the prompt girl to stand behind the curtain, immediately behind Vi as I was certain she'd dry – and she did, but even when the girl gave her the lines she didn't do anything. She'd frozen to the spot. Her ears had gone bright blue and her neck was going dark red. I thought she was going to have a heart attack. I started to say her lines for her, grasped her hand and helped her through, she and I doing a bit each. It was obvious to everyone that she'd frozen, but we muddled through it. She was wet through with terror.

We'd all been told to ignore the Queen and the Duke of Edinburgh sitting in the Royal Box but when it came to Peter Adamson, who played Len Fairclough, he delivered all his lines to them and kept winking at them. After the show finished we all stood outside the entrance to the Royal Box to be presented. Jean and Jack Howarth were picked to go into the Box to greet the Queen and lead her out to the rest of us. Jean practised her curtsy for weeks, with me standing in the dressing room being the Queen. She bought a new dress for the occasion, full length, bright emerald green with a great big sunburst of gold sequins on the front. They went into the Royal Box and Jean did her curtsy, just like a cavalier, very deep and low. She might as well have had a hat with a plume in it! Somehow her foot stuck in her frock. She tripped and shot forward and the Queen had to grab her to save her from falling over the edge of the box. I was standing in the doorway and couldn't believe my eyes. Poor Jean! She was all flustered. When the party came out the Queen looked at me and said, 'Oh, my feet hurt so much,' and all I could think of to say was, 'Oh, I am sorry!' The Duke of Edinburgh said, 'Have you got a pint or a cup of tea?' I said, 'No, sorry.'

Then in 1982 I met the Queen and the Duke again when they opened the new outside *Street* set. I had to stand outside the Rovers with Doris and Julie to be introduced to them. Julie had had some big earrings made, one of Charles, one of Diana. I thought that was very tacky but she said, 'They'll notice them.' She curtsied to the Queen, gestured to her ears and said, 'I even know which side of the bed they sleep.' The Queen gave her a cold look and said, 'Really.' They moved on to Doris, who had refused to put in her hearing-aid and the Queen spoke very quietly. Doris said, 'What did you say, dear?' I nearly kicked her off the step! I had to explain to the Queen that she was a bit deaf. I couldn't believe it when, once again, the Duke asked me if I had anything to drink. I must have looked as if I was hiding a tea urn or something!

I was reminded of that official opening of the Street eighteen years later when I collected my M.B.E. I was so thrilled when I learnt I was to be honoured and on 7 March 2000 lined up with the other worthies. Needless to say I was nervous when we arrived at the Palace as I was separated from Freda who went to sit in the audience with my agent Morris and the Street's historian Daran Little. I wanted to go with them but wasn't allowed so I sat and chatted to Nobby Styles who was also getting the M.B.E. When my time came to walk into the ballroom at Buckingham Palace I concentrated on not wobbling as I curtseyed and was presented with my medal. The Queen said, 'We came to open your Street. Do you still use it?' It was a beautiful occasion and I felt very proud of myself.

It's not very often I travel to London these days and my M.B.E visit was made all the more special by Charles Allen, Granada's Chief Executive. He is a great fan of the *Street* and always takes an interest in us actors. He arranged a beautiful suite at the Grosvenor House Hotel for us to stay in, brimming with deep red roses, platters of fresh fruit and champagne – to settle the nerves! It's kindnesses like these that make all the difference.

I'm fortunate enough to do both comedy and drama in the *Street* but I have to say I prefer doing the comedy. Personally, I feel there aren't enough people in it at the moment who can time gags. Barbara is the best gag-timer in the business, but she used to work as a feed with the likes of Les Dawson and Ken Dodd. I learnt my timing from standing in the wings watching the greats at work. In the old days of the show we could afford to record scenes where nothing happened, just sitting around talking. I miss those scenes. I know pubs. The Rovers isn't a posh place, it's homely, and everyone who comes in is known. Therefore there'd be many more general conversations, involving everyone in the bar. It should be ringing with laughter more. Laughter . . . that's the key.

CHAPTER SIXTEEN

My Best Friend

Hotpot has become my trademark, and the trademark for the whole show – more so than Bet's earrings, Ena's hairnet or even Hilda's curlers. It's amazing. Everywhere I go people ask me for hotpot. We were in Monte Carlo once, walking along by the sea, and this well-dressed man stood up from a table outside a café, tipped his hat and asked, 'How is your hotpot today?' It happens everywhere I go. The ironic thing is I don't actually eat hotpot because I don't eat meat, just chicken and fish. I think it's ridiculous me being linked to hotpot! I've even got my face on a range of hotpots and pies manufactured by Holland's called 'Betty's Kitchen'. They're sold in supermarkets and I know they're tasty, because I had to taste them myself.

The tasting was at the end of a long day I'm never likely to forget. I'd been invited to view the factory where they were made and took along Freda and our good friend Charles Orr. Charles is a florist and is part of a small band of men who are Freda's and my dearest friends. There's Michael Clowes, a chef, Mark Hudson, Director of Studies at the Sheena Simon College in Manchester, computer expert Brian Lynch, and Charles. The three of us went to Accrington, tarted up with jewels, ready for a Personal Appearance. We were introduced to the MD and given coffee, then the works manager asked us to take all our jewellery off and locked it in a safe. They asked what size shoes we took and produced these white wellington boots. Now I take a size seven but they didn't have a pair for me so I had to wear a larger size. I could have got two feet into each boot! I'd started off full of myself, having these hotpots made for me, but I was soon forced down to earth. Next came the coats – large white lab coats that covered our clothes. I looked like an ice cream vendor; Freda looked like the Grim Reaper. Next came the white hairnets which had to cover all our hair and ears, then finally yellow hard hats. By this time I was hysterical. My hat was too small, Freda's too big and Charles looked as if he had a pimple on his head. We had a two-hour tour, and before going into each part of the factory we had to wash our hands. Six times we had to wash our hands. Then we had to walk through disinfected water in our wellies and when we went through the raw meat department we had to change the colour of our coats and were given red ones. Mine was slightly flared. Every inch of my cool had gone but by that stage I didn't care what I looked like. Every time I walked my wellies blew raspberries, and I was sweating so much the hairnet stuck to the hair spray I'd applied that morning and I couldn't take it off! Afterwards they filled the boot of my car with pies and hotpots. Our friends lived off it for months!

I've only known Charles, Michael, Mark and Brian a relatively short time so none of them appeared on my *This Is Your Life* back in 1976. Freda, of course, planned the whole thing and had to get me down on the train to Euston where the 'grab' was to take place. Freda said we were going to a champion dog show and she had to keep me trapped in the train, pretending she'd lost her gloves, until everyone else had got off. Then she walked me down the platform and there was Eamonn Andrews done up like a news vendor with a huge newspaper board on which was written 'Big Surprise for Betty Driver'. I was stunned! All I can remember was worrying that they'd bring my husband out! Of course, Freda had seen to it that they didn't but lovely Jack Watson came on, and Beryl Reid, and – to my absolute horror – Lena Brown, the whistling woman from *Let's Be Famous*. When she came on I nearly had a heart attack. Goodness knows where they'd dug her up from!

Freda sat next to me during my *This Is Your Life* and, of course, that's where she's always been, next to me, holding my hand through the bad times. I cannot really put into words just what my sister means to me. She's sacrificed so much for me, and has always put my interests before her own. She's kept me going. Without her I'd have hidden myself away years ago in a remote cottage somewhere. I've been fortunate because there's the two of us. We are the best of friends, do everything together, and apart from seven years, we've been all each other has had for seventy-seven years. When I was a little girl I dreamt of being a hairdresser. Then I wanted my own florist shop or a garden centre. I didn't want to be on the stage. Standing on a deserted stage belting out songs to a sea of faces sitting in the dark was too lonely, but that was my lot. Without Freda, though, I could never have carried on after my marriage, and I would never have had the drive to join the *Street*.

Freda looks after every area of my life. She even chooses what car I drive. At the moment it's a Honda. I wanted a black car with a black lining but Freda said I should have a cream lining so that's what I've got. Soft cream pure leather. I go to a dress shop in Nantwich in Cheshire, which has glorious clothes, and after I've kissed all the assistants I sit in one of the cubicles and Freda goes round the shop choosing what I'm going to try on. If ever I do buy clothes on my own I get all excited and try them on at home and Freda just stares at me. And she's right, I always look a dreadful fright and they all go back to the shop or I give them away, often with the price tags still in them. Freda knows exactly what clothes complement me. All my life I've always been asking her, 'What do you think, Freda? Which should I have, Freda?' In the theatre, in my dressing-room, I'd panic over what to wear and ask her for guidance and sometimes she'd shrug and say, 'Wear what you like. They're all lovely gowns – put on the one you want to wear' and I'd just stare at the row of dresses. Eventually I'd say, 'If you don't tell me I won't go on!' I have no confidence in myself at all. My only confidence is on-screen. There, at work, I have 100 per cent confidence, but within myself I have no time for me at all. There was a time when I'd make the odd personal appearance, but only if I had Freda with me. I can't bear it when people crowd around me for autographs: it makes me feel so scared. It's only natural that people gather, but I feel like I can't breathe. I don't like it but I can just about cope with it if Freda's with me. I'd face the Devil if she sat beside me.

I know at work people must think I'm awfully strange because I sit alone in my dressing room and don't really socialize with the newer cast members. I think they see me as a strange woman who only appears in the Green Room to phone this mysterious Freda eight times a day! I love my dressing room: I have a television in it and at lunchtime I sit there watching *Home and Away* and *Jerry Springer* and I have my radio and a fridge and I do my tapestry. A place of my own. It's sandwiched between Barbara and Helen, across the way from Eileen and Bill. We pop in and out of each other's rooms all the time for a chat and the first thing they ask is, 'How's Freda?'

My last word should really be in explaining why I've written this book. I've already said that I'm a private person and I lack confidence in myself. I'm using my eightieth birthday as an excuse to write my story but have to admit I've been avoiding it for years. *Coronation Street*'s archivist, Daran Little, has been badgering me to write my autobiography for far too long and I've always put him off, but then something happened in the summer of 1999. Freda had a dream in which she remembered us visiting an airfield during the war. The morning after the dream Daran phoned up and threw us completely by telling us he'd made an exciting discovery. The dream and the discovery were the same thing and it's a tale that takes us back to 1942.

Freda and I were two carefree girls being driven in the back of a dusty old army truck along roads and dirt tracks. It was a bumpy journey, and a long one. We had no idea where we were going, National Security saw to that. In fact, as we staggered out of the truck and blinked in the sunlight we recognized the landscape and calculated we had spent nearly two hours driving round and round in circles to travel less than five miles.

Our destination was an airfield, and we were met by Richard Murdoch of the RAF and a leading light in ENSA. We'd never met him before but knew him from his radio broadcasts as Stinker Murdoch, the straight man who played opposite Arthur Askey in *Band Wagon*. I was one of a long line of entertainers visiting the camp, and everyone who booked me for anything knew I didn't go anywhere without 'our Freda'. We were stylish young ladies and fancied ourselves rotten in our smart outfits and hats. We saw ourselves as bringing glamour into the lives of these servicemen, but we were soon brought down to earth when led past trenches beside the runway.

'What are those for?' I asked Stinker.

'If the Germans fly over you'll hear a whistle blowing. Run like mad to a trench and jump into it,' he said cheerfully.

Freda and I exchanged a weak smile. I couldn't imagine doing any leaping in my tight skirt.

Inside a huge hangar, engineers at the camp were working on constructing aircraft using new combustion engines. Having decided we weren't enemy spies we were shown the two planes they were working on. They were small and light, and Freda and I made such a fuss about them that the commanding officer announced that they would be named after us. We were delighted but, such was the excitement of war, we soon forgot all about them.

Over fifty years later, Daran was out with his sons visiting Manchester's Air and Space Museum, just two hundred yards from the *Coronation Street* studio. They chanced upon two shiny combustion engines, one named Betty, the other Freda. The sparkling new aircraft we had watched being built had long since gone for scrap but the engines, our engines, were still intact. They had survived, and so, I realized, had their namesakes. If you ever visit the museum seek those engines out: if you've enjoyed my story you've got them to thank for it being written.

Discography

Recording date	Title	78 issue number
4 May 1935	Jubilee Baby (Dodd)	Regal Zonophone MR 1703
4 May 1935	The Little Woolly Vest (Jackson, Aza)	Regal Zonophone MR 1703
4 May 1935	The Alpine Milkman (Sarony)	Regal Zonophone MR 1704
4 May 1935	It's Men Like You (unknown)	Regal Zonophone MR 1704
3 January 1938	I'm Getting Sentimental Over You (Bassman, Washington)	vocal test (unissued)
3 January 1938	The Ghost of the Barber Sweeney Todd (Maysie, Bean, Stuart)	vocal test (unissued)
18 February 1938	I'm Getting Sentimental Over You (Bassman, Washington)	HMV BD 530
18 February 1938	With You (Smith, Walters)	HMV BD 530
5 April 1938	I Love to Whistle (McHugh, Adamson)	HMV BD 545

Recording date	Title	78 issue number
5 April 1938	I'll Take Romance (Hammerstein II, Oakland)	HMV BD 545
6 May 1938	The Sweetest Song in the World (Parr Davies)	HMV BD 556
6 May 1938	I Fall in Love With You Every Day (Sherwin, Loesser)	HMV BD 556
10 June 1938	So Little Time (De Rose, Hill)	HMV BD 575
10 June 1938	Oh Ma-Ma! (The Butcher Boy) (Brown, Citorello, Vallee)	HMV BD 575
11 October 1938	What Goes on Here in My Heart? (Robin, Rainger)	HMV BD 605
11 October 1938	Red Maple Leaves (Kennedy, Grosz)	HMV BD 605
30 March 1939	Waltz of My Heart (Hassall, Novello)	HMV BD 5479
30 March 1939	I Can Give You the Starlight (intro. The Leap Year Waltz) (Hassall, Novello)	HMV BD 5479
30 March 1939	The Moon Remembered (But You Forgot) (Eyton, Gay)	HMV BD 686
30 March 1939	I've Got a Hunch (Eyton, Gay)	HMV BD 686
13 January 1942	Swing Bugler (Campbell, Park, Thompson)	Regal Zonophone MR 3593
13 January 1942	The World Will Sing Again (Day, Ralton, Miller)	Regal Zonophone MR 3593

Discography

Recording date	Title	78 issue number
1 September 1942	Medley: (a) The Sailor With the Navy Blue Eyes (Taylor, Mizzy, Hoffman) (b) It's Spring Again (Noel) (c) Potato Pete (Miller, Charles)	Regal Zonophone MR 3657
1 September 1942	Medley: (a) What More Can I Say? (Noel) (b) The Booglie Wooglie Piggie (Jacobs) (c) Rose O'Day (Tobias, Lewis)	Regal Zonophone MR 3657
10 December 1942	We Mustn't Miss the Last Bus Home (Butler, Gay)	Regal Zonophone MR 3674
10 December 1942	Twitterpated (Bliss, Sour, Manners)	Regal Zonophone MR 3674
12 September 1949	Monday, Tuesday, Wednesday (I Love You) (Parker)	HMV B 9825
12 September 1949	The Bullfrog (Samba) (Norman, Munn)	HMV B 9825
12 September 1949	Leprechaun Lullaby (Hulbert)	HMV B 9834
12 September 1949	A Dreamer's Holiday (Wayne, Gannon)	HMV B 9834
16 December 1950	Red Silken Stockings (Hart, Brandon)	HMV BD 6086

Recording date	Title	78 issue number
June 1954	Let's Gather Round the Old Parlour Piano (McHugh, Adamson)	Planet E 1012
June 1954	I Know You're Mine (Murrells)	Planet E 1012

Note: Some sources claim that Betty Driver made recordings of 'MacNamara's Band', 'Pick the Petals Off A Daisy' and 'September in the Rain', but none of these can be verified from official sources. In addition to the titles listed in this discography, the BBC Sound Archive holds two recordings of live broadcasts made by Betty Driver: *Variety Bandbox* (1949), in which she sings 'Leicester Square Rag', and the twenty-first birthday edition of *Henry Hall's Guest Night* (1955), in which she sings 'The Sailor With the Navy Blue Eyes'.

Career Highlights

1930 at the age of nine won a Gold Medal in a talent contest and joined the Terence Byron Repertory Company in Longsight, Manchester

1931 toured in the revue *Mixed Bathing*

1932 at the age of twelve sang for the first time on BBC radio

1934 made film debut in *Boots! Boots!* with George Formby but Betty's cabaret number was cut from the release print on the instruction of Formby's wife Beryl

1934 made first London stage appearance in a variety show at the Prince of Wales Theatre

1934–36 toured in the revue *Mr Tower of London* with Norman Evans

1935 made first recording at the age of fourteen (*Jubilee Baby*) and continued recording until 1954

1936 appeared in Jimmy Hunter's *Brighton Follies* for a summer season in Brighton

1937 appeared at the Adelphi Theatre in London's West End in Charles B. Cochran's revue *Home and Beauty*

1938 co-starred with Edmund Gwenn and Jimmy O'Dea in the film *Penny Paradise* directed by Carol Reed

1938 appeared at the Blackpool Opera House in the revue *All the Best* with Anton Dolin, Stanley Holloway and Elisabeth Welch

1939 co-starred with Jimmy O'Dea and Sonnie Hale in the film *Let's Be Famous* directed by Walter Forde

1940 featured in the wartime film short *The American Eagle Club*

1941 co-starred with Bunny Doyle in the film *Facing the Music* directed by MacLean Rogers

1941–48 featured vocalist with Henry Hall and his BBC Dance Orchestra in the long-running BBC radio series *Henry Hall's Guest Night*

During the Second World War entertained the troops in France, Belgium, Germany, Holland and North Africa with Henry Hall for ENSA

1945 performed with Henry Hall on the Champs Elysées in Paris on VE night

1949 starred in her own BBC radio series *A Date with Betty* on the Light Programme

1950 made an early television appearance for the BBC in *Rooftop Rendevous*

1952 starred in her own BBC television series *The Betty Driver Show*

1952 co-starred with Arthur Askey, Tommy Cooper, Frankie Howerd and Norman Wisdom in *Television's Second Christmas Party*, an all-star variety show broadcast on BBC television on Christmas Day

1957 made a guest appearance in BBC television's *The Good Old Days*

1960 co-starred with Glenn Melvyn and Danny Ross in the comedy *Pillar to Post* at the Blackpool Grand Theatre

1961 co-starred with Arthur Askey and Beatrice Varley in the comedy *What A Racket!* at the Blackpool Grand Theatre

1965–68 co-starred with Arthur Lowe in Granada television's *Coronation Street* spin-off comedy series *Pardon the Expression*

1967 played a supporting role in the Granada television play *Love on the Dole* with Anne Stallybrass and James Bolam

1969 joined the cast of Granada television's *Coronation Street* on 2 June

1976 subject of *This is Your Life* for Thames Television

1978 made guest appearance in *Looks Familiar* for Thames Television

1986 subject of BBC Radio 2's *It's a Funny Business*

1987 presented with a Gold Badge of Merit by BASCA (British Academy of Songwriters, Composers and Arrangers) in recognition of her services to British music

1988 made guest appearance on *Wogan* for BBC television

1989 made guest appearance with the cast of *Coronation Street* in the Royal Variety Performance, later televised by London Weekend Television

1989 paid tribute to Henry Hall in BBC Radio 2's tribute *Here's to the Next Time*

1992 appeared in *The South Bank Show: George Formby* for London Weekend Television

1994 subject of BBC Radio 2's *The Betty Driver Story* presented by Cilla Black

1999 celebrated thirty years in *Coronation Street* and listed as the third-longest serving member of the cast behind William Roache (Ken Barlow) and Eileen Derbyshire (Emily Bishop)

2000 awarded MBE in New Year's Honours List and publication of autobiography to coincide with eightieth birthday on May 20

Acknowledgements

With thanks to my sister, Freda, Morris Aza, my agent and good friend, and Daran Little for all their help with the book. Thanks are also due to Andrew G. Marshall, Roy Hudd, Stephen Bourne, Richard Anthony Baker, Richard Mangan at Mander & Mitchenson Theatre Collection, Johnnie and Violet Riscoe for additional research; Stephen Bourne for the career highlights and Stephen Bourne, Hugh Palmer and David Rolfe for the discography.

Picture Acknowledgements

Thanks to Neil Marland for taking the new pictures of Freda and myself.

The photographs on the back cover and on page 8, top, of the plate section are reproduced courtesy of the BBC. The photographs on page 13, bottom, and pages 13 to 16 of the plate section are reproduced courtesy of Granada Media.

The author and publishers have made every responsible effort to contact all copyright holders. Any errors that may have occurred are inadvertent and anyone who for any reason has not been contacted is invited to write to the publishers so that a full acknowledgement may be made in subsequent editions of this work.

Index